HOUGHTON MIFFLIN
Reading
A Legacy of Literacy

W9-COE-263

Florida Teacher's Edition
Kindergarten

Senior Authors J. David Cooper, John J. Pikulski

Authors Patricia A. Ackerman, Kathryn H. Au, David J. Chard, Gilbert G. Garcia, Claude N. Goldenberg, Marjorie Y. Lipson, Susan E. Page, Shane Templeton, Sheila W. Valencia, MaryEllen Vogt

Consultants Linda H. Butler, Linnea C. Ehri, Carla B. Ford

Florida Consultants Shirley Payne Fields, Patricia F. Nelms, Connie Shaffer

HOUGHTON MIFFLIN   BOSTON • MORRIS PLAINS, NJ

California • Colorado • Georgia • Illinois • New Jersey • Texas

Florida Program Reviewers

Faye Blake, Jacksonville; **Suzi Boyett**,Sarasota; **Patti Brustad**,Sarasota; **Jan Buckelew**, Venice; **Jennifer Davison**, West Palm Beach; **Merry Guest**, Homestead; **Coleen Howard-Whals**, St. Petersburg; **Beverly Hurst**, Jacksonville; **Debra Jackson**, St. Petersburg; **Cheryl Kellogg**, Panama City; **Ileana Masud**, Miami; **David Miller**, Cooper City; **Marina Rodriguez**, Hialeah; **Linda Schrum**, Orlando; **Sharon Searcy**, Mandarin; **Melba Sims**, Orlando; **Judy Smith**, Titusville; **Beverley Wakefield**, Tarpon Springs; **Marti Watson**, Sarasota

Literature Reviewers

Consultants: **Dr. Adela Artola Allen**, Associate Dean, Graduate College, Associate Vice President for Inter-American Relations, University of Arizona, Tucson, Arizona; **Dr. Manley Begay**, Co-director of the Harvard Project on American Indian Economic Development, Director of the National Executive Education Program for Native Americans, Harvard University, John F. Kennedy School of Government, Cambridge, Massachusetts; **Dr. Nicholas Kannellos**, Director, Arte Publico Press, Director, Recovering the U.S. Hispanic Literacy Heritage Project, University of Houston, Texas; **Mildred Lee**, author and former head of Library Services for Sonoma County, Santa Rosa, California; **Dr. Barbara Moy**, Director of the Office of Communication Arts, Detroit Public Schools, Michigan; **Norma Naranjo**, Clark County School District, Las Vegas, Nevada; **Dr. Arlette Ingram Willis**, Associate Professor, Department of Curriculum and Instruction, Division of Language and Literacy, University of Illinois at Urbana-Champaign, Illinois

Teachers: **Helen Brooks**, Vestavia Hills Elementary School, Birmingham, Alabama; **Patricia Buchanan**, Thurgood Marshall School, Newark, Delaware; **Gail Connor**, Language Arts Resource Teacher, Duval County, Jacksonville, Florida; **Vicki DeMott**, McClean Science/Technology School, Wichita, Kansas; **Marge Egenhoffer**, Dixon Elementary School, Brookline, Wisconsin; **Mary Jew Mori**, Griffin Avenue Elementary, Los Angeles, California

ESOL Reviewers

Manuel Brenes, Michigan; **Tim Fornier**, Michigan; **Anna Lugo**, Illinois; **Carolyn Mason**, Washington; **Ileana Masud**, Florida; **Marina Rodriguez**, Florida; **Noemi Velazquez**, New Jersey; **Dr. Santiago Veve**, Nevada

Printed in the U.S.A.

ISBN: 0-618-15732-8

2 3 4 5 6 7 8 9-B-07 06 05 04 03 02

Credits

Cover
Copyright © Michio Hoshino/Minden Pictures

Theme Opener
(t) (b) copyright © Frans Lanting/Minden Pictures, (m) copyright © Michio Hoshino/Minden Pictures

Photography
StockByte
p. T89

Assignment Photography
Joel Benjamin
pp. xiv, T9, T13, T21, T23, T32, T43, T67, T75, T77, T88, T99, T123, T127, T131, T149

Illustration
Salvatore Murdocca, p. T65; Don Stuart, p. T121

Acknowledgments

Grateful acknowledgment is made for permission to reprint copyrighted material as follows:

Theme 10
Splash, by Flora McDonnell. Copyright © 1999 by Flora McDonnell. Reproduced by permission of Candlewick Press, Cambridge, MA.

Feathers for Lunch, by Lois Ehlert. Copyright © 1990 by Lois Ehlert. Reprinted by permission of Harcourt, Inc.

Correlation to the Sunshine State Standards

Skills	Sunshine State Standards

Reading

Phonemic Awareness/Phonics/Decoding

Skills	Sunshine State Standards
Phonemic Awareness: Blending and Segmenting Phonemes, *TE:T9, T17, T27, T39, T47, T61, T71, T81, T95, T103, T117, T127, T137, T145, T153*	★ **LA.A.1.1.2.K.5** understands basic phonetic principles.
Phonemic Awareness: Phoneme Substitution, *TE:T9, T17, T27, T39, T47, T61, T71, T81, T95, T103, T117, T127, T137, T145, T153*	★ **LA.A.1.1.2.K.5** understands basic phonetic principles.
Initial Consonant *j, TE:T12–T13, T20–T21*	★ **LA.A.1.1.2.K.3** knows the sounds of the letters of the alphabet. ★ **LA.A.1.1.2.K.5** understands basic phonetic principles.
Initial Consonants *d, j, n,* and *w, TE:T122–T123, T130–T131*	★ **LA.A.1.1.2.K.3** knows the sounds of the letters of the alphabet. ★ **LA.A.1.1.2.K.5** understands basic phonetic principles.
Blending *-ug* words, *TE:T34, T42–T43, T67, T74, T92, T100, T106, T108, T140, T148–T149*	★ **LA.A.1.1.2.K.5** understands basic phonetic principles. ★ **LA.A.1.1.3.K.4** uses a variety of sources to build vocabulary.
Blending *-ut* words, *TE:T90, T98–T99, T100, T106, T108, T140, T148–T149, T156, T158*	★ **LA.A.1.1.2.K.5** understands basic phonetic principles. ★ **LA.A.1.1.3.K.4** uses a variety of sources to build vocabulary.
Phonics Review: Familiar Consonants; *-ug, -et, -en* words, *TE:T13, T20, T36, T44, T50, T52, T67, T74, T92, T100, T106, T108, T123, T130, T142, T156, T158*	★ **LA.A.1.1.2.K.3** knows the sounds of the letters of the alphabet. ★ **LA.A.1.1.2.K.5** understands basic phonetic principles. ★ **LA.A.1.1.3.K.4** uses a variety of sources to build vocabulary.

High-Frequency Words

Skills	Sunshine State Standards
High-Frequency Words, *TE:T8, T16, T26, T38, T46, T76–T77, T91, T107, T132–T133, T141, T157*	★ **LA.A.1.1.3.K.1** identifies frequently used words.
Word Wall, *TE:T8, T16, T26, T38, T46, T60, T70, T80, T94, T102, T116, T126, T136, T144, T152*	★ **LA.A.1.1.3.K.1** identifies frequently used words. ★ **LA.A.1.1.3.K.4** uses a variety of sources to build vocabulary.

Comprehension Skills and Strategies

Skills	Sunshine State Standards
Strategies: Question, *TE:T10, T18, T29, T40*	**LA.A.1.1.4.K.1** uses strategies to comprehend text.
Strategies: Predict/Infer, *TE:T62, T72, T83, T86, T96*	**LA.A.1.1.1.K.1** uses titles and illustrations to make oral predictions. **LA.A.1.1.4.K.1** uses strategies to comprehend text.
Strategies: Summarize, *TE:T118, T128, T129, T138*	**LA.A.1.1.4.K.1** uses strategies to comprehend text.
Strategies: Phonics/Decoding, *TE:T35, T91, T141*	★ **LA.A.1.1.2.K.3** knows the sounds of the letters of the alphabet. ★ **LA.A.1.1.2.K.4** understands the concept of words and constructs meaning from shared text, illustrations, graphics, and charts. ★ **LA.A.1.1.2.K.5** understands basic phonetic principles.
Comprehension: Story Structure: Beginning, Middle, End, *TE:T10, T18, T29, T30, T31, T46*	★ **LA.E.1.1.2.K.1** knows the sequence of events, characters, and setting of stories **LA.C.1.1.4.K.1** listens for specific information, including sequence of events.
Comprehension: Compare and Contrast, *TE:T62, T72, T83, T84, T85, T96, T104*	★ **Sunshine State Standards for Grades K–2 do not include this skill as a Benchmark. It is an FCAT Benchmark in Grades 3–5.**
Comprehension: Story Structure: Plot, *TE:T118, T128, T129, T138, T139, T154*	★ **LA.E.1.1.2.K.1** knows the sequence of events, characters, and setting of stories

Word Work

High-Frequency Word Practice

Skills	Sunshine State Standards
Matching Words, *TE:T14, T68, T124*	★ **LA.A.1.1.3.K.1** identifies frequently used words.
Building Sentences, *TE:T24, T78, T134*	★ **LA.A.1.1.2.K.4** understands the concept of words and constructs meaning from shared text, illustrations, graphics, and charts.

continued

★ = *FCAT Benchmark in Gr. 3–5*   *TE = Teacher's Edition*

Skills	Sunshine State Standards

Word Work *continued*

Building Words

Building Words: Word Family -ug, *TE:T36, T44, T52, T100, T108, T142, T150, T158*	★ **LA.A.1.1.2.K.4** understands the concept of words and constructs meaning from shared text, illustrations, graphics, and charts. ★ **LA.A.1.1.2.K.5** understands basic phonetic principles. ★ **LA.A.1.1.3.K.4** uses a variety of sources to build vocabulary.
Building Words: Word Family -ut, *TE:T92, T100, T108, T142, T150, T158*	★ **LA.A.1.1.2.K.4** understands the concept of words and constructs meaning from shared text, illustrations, graphics, and charts. ★ **LA.A.1.1.2.K.5** understands basic phonetic principles. ★ **LA.A.1.1.3.K.4** uses a variety of sources to build vocabulary.
Building Words: Word Families -ug, -ut, -et, -en, -ot, *TE:T46, T54, T100, T108, T142, T150, T158*	★ **LA.A.1.1.2.K.4** understands the concept of words and constructs meaning from shared text, illustrations, graphics, and charts. ★ **LA.A.1.1.2.K.5** understands basic phonetic principles. ★ **LA.A.1.1.3.K.4** uses a variety of sources to build vocabulary.

Writing and Language

Oral Language

Using Exact Naming Words: Animal Names Chart, *TE:T15*	★ **LA.A.1.1.3.K.2** identifies words that name persons, places, or things and words that name actions.
Using Rhyming Words: Rhyming Chart, *TE:T69*	**LA.D.2.1.2.K.1** uses repetition, rhyme, and rhythm in oral and written texts.
Using Order Words: Order Words Chart, *TE:T125*	**LA.D.2.1.2.K.1** uses repetition, rhyme, and rhythm in oral and written texts.
Comparing Information, *TE:T25*	**LA.C.1.1.4.K.1** listens for specific information, including sequence of events.
Using Exact Words, Rhyming Words, *TE:T79*	★ **LA.A.1.1.2.K.5** understands basic phonetic principles. ★ **LA.A.1.1.3.K.4** uses a variety of sources to build vocabulary.
Animal Names, *TE:T135*	★ **LA.A.1.1.3.K.2** identifies words that name persons, places, or things and words that name actions.

Writing

Shared Writing: Writing a Report, *TE:T37*	**LA.B.1.1.3.K.3** identifies and attempts to use end punctuation. **LA.B.2.1.1.K.2** contributes ideas during a shared writing activity. **LA.B.2.1.2.K.1** dictates and writes with pictures or words to record ideas and reflections.
Shared Writing: Writing a Book Report, *TE:T93*	**LA.B.2.1.1.K.2** contributes ideas during a shared writing activity. **LA.B.2.1.2.K.1** dictates and writes with pictures or words to record ideas and reflections. **LA.E.2.1.1.K.1** relates characters and simple events in a read-aloud book to own life.
Shared Writing: Writing Directions, *TE:T143*	★ **LA.A.1.1.2.K.1** understands how print is organized and read. **LA.B.1.1.2.K.3** demonstrates ability to sequence events during shared writing exercises. **LA.B.2.1.1.K.2** contributes ideas during a shared writing activity. **LA.B.2.1.4.K.1** dictates or writes simple informational texts.
Interactive Writing: Writing a Report, *TE:T45*	**LA.B.1.1.3.K.3** identifies and attempts to use end punctuation. **LA.B.2.1.1.K.1** dictates or writes with pictures or words a narrative about a familiar experience. **LA.B.2.1.1.K.2** contributes ideas during a shared writing activity.
Interactive Writing: Writing a Book Report, *TE:T101*	**LA.B.2.1.2.K.1** dictates and writes with pictures or words to record ideas and reflections. **LA.E.2.1.1.K.1** relates characters and simple events in a read-aloud book to own life.
Interactive Writing: Writing Directions, *TE:T151*	**LA.B.1.1.2.K.1** dictates messages (for example, news, stories) **LA.B.1.1.2.K.3** demonstrates ability to sequence events during shared writing exercises. **LA.B.2.1.4.K.1** dictates or writes simple informational texts.
Independent Writing: Journals, *TE:T55, T109, T159*	**LA.B.2.1.1.K.1** dictates or writes with pictures or words a narrative about a familiar experience. **LA.B.2.1.2.K.1** dictates and writes with pictures or words to record ideas and reflections. **LA.E.2.1.1.K.1** relates characters and simple events in a read-aloud book to own life.

Listening/Speaking/Viewing

Listening, *TE:T25*	**LA.C.1.1.4.K.1** listens for specific information, including sequence of events.
Viewing and Speaking, *TE:T37*	**LA.C.2.1.1.K.1** understands the main idea in a nonprint communication. **LA.C.3.1.3.K.1** uses basic speaking vocabulary to convey a message in conversation.
Listening, Speaking, and Viewing, *TE:T45*	**LA.C.1.1.4.K.1** listens for specific information, including sequence of events. **LA.C.2.1.1.K.1** understands the main idea in a nonprint communication. **LA.C.3.1.2.K.1** asks and responds to questions.
Listening and Viewing, *TE:T79*	**LA.C.1.1.4.K.1** listens for specific information, including sequence of events. **LA.C.2.1.1.K.1** understands the main idea in a nonprint communication.
Viewing and Speaking, *TE:T93*	**LA.C.2.1.1.K.1** understands the main idea in a nonprint communication. **LA.C.3.1.3.K.1** uses basic speaking vocabulary to convey a message in conversation.
Listening, Viewing, and Speaking, *TE:T101*	**LA.C.1.1.4.K.1** listens for specific information, including sequence of events. **LA.C.2.1.1.K.1** understands the main idea in a nonprint communication.
Viewing, *TE:T135*	**LA.C.2.1.1.K.1** understands the main idea in a nonprint communication.

For Cross-Curricular correlations, see individual activities.

★ = FCAT Benchmark in Gr. 3–5   TE = Teacher's Edition

Theme 10

A World of Animals

Phonemic Awareness blending and segmenting phonemes; phoneme substitution

Phonics sound for letters *J, j;* review letters *b, c, d, j, l, n, w*

Decoding *-ug* and *-ut* word families

High-Frequency Words recognize two new high-frequency words

Reading Strategies question; predict/infer; summarize; phonics/decoding

Comprehension Skills story structure: beginning, middle, end; compare and contrast; story structure: plot

Vocabulary exact naming words; comparing information; rhyming words; order words; animal names

Writing report; journals; book report; directions

Listening/Speaking/Viewing activities to support vocabulary expansion and writing

Theme 10

A World of Animals
Literature Resources

Big Books for Use All Year

From Apples to
Zebras:
A Book of ABC's

Higglety Pigglety:
A Book of Rhymes

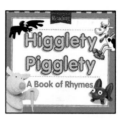

Fun in the Sun:
A Big Book of Florida

Leveled Books

See Cumulative Listing of Leveled Books.

Phonics Library

Very Easy

- Ken and Jen
- It Can Fit
- The Bug Hut

Lessons,
pages T35, T91,
T141

On My Way Practice Reader

Easy / On Level

Animals at Play

by Wil Perry
page T155

Little Big Books

On Level / Challenge

Splash!

Feathers
for Lunch

📼 Audiotape

A World of Animals

Houghton Mifflin Classroom Bookshelf

Level K

Little Readers for Guided Reading

Collection K

Bibliography

Books for Browsing

 Animal ABC's
by the World Wildlife Fund
Cedco 1997 (28p)
Stunning color photographs show animals of the land and sea for each letter of the alphabet.

Sweet Dreams
by Kimiko Kajikawa
Holt 1999 (32p)
Simple rhyming verse describes the many different ways animals sleep.

A Kitten's Year
by Nancy Raines Day
Harper 2000 (32p)
A kitten paws and pounces its way through the months of a year.

 I Had a Hippopotamus
by Hector Viveros Lee
Lee & Low 1998 (32p) paper
A boy imagines what he would do with the creatures in his box of animal crackers. **Available in Spanish as Yo tenía un hipopótamo.**

Animals in the Fall
by Gail Saunders-Smith
Pebble 1998 (24p) also paper
In autumn, geese fly south, bears find dens, and squirrels build nests.

 Giant Pandas
by Marcia S. Freeman
Pebble 1999 (24p)
Simple text and photos describe the giant panda, a native of China, and its behavior.

 Tabby
by Aliki
Harper 1995 (32p)
In this wordless story, a kitten's first year with its new family is one of growth and exploration.

Little Lions
 by Jim Arnosky
Putnam 1998 (32p)
On a rocky ledge, two mountain lion cubs play under the protection of their mother.

I Love Animals
by Flora McDonnell
Candlewick 1994 (32p)
From dogs and ducks to pigs and ponies, a girl tells about the farm animals she loves.

Books for Teacher Read Aloud

 Whistle for Willie
by Ezra Jack Keats
Viking 1964 (32p) also paper
An African American boy learns to whistle for his dog. **Available in Spanish as Sílbale a Willie.**

 Blueberries for Sal
by Robert McCloskey
Viking 1948 (56p) also paper
Picking blueberries on a hillside, a girl and a bear cub have a surprise meeting.

Ducks Don't Get Wet
by Augusta Goldin
Harper 1999 (32p) also paper
Wild ducks can swim in the water without getting wet. See others in series.

 Harry the Dirty Dog
by Gene Zion
Harper 1956 (32p) also paper
The classic story about a dog, some dirt, and a bath. **Available in Spanish as Harry, el perrito sucio.**

The Mitten
by Jan Brett
Putnam 1989 (32p)
A rabbit, an owl, a fox, and even a bear all squeeze into a boy's lost mitten in this Ukrainian folktale.

 *Henny Penny
by Paul Galdone
Clarion 1968 (32p) also paper
Convinced the sky is falling, Henny Penny and her friends rush off to tell the king.

 Coyote
by Gerald McDermott
Harcourt (32p) also paper
Coyote persuades some crows to help him fly in this Native American trickster tale.
Available in Spanish as Coyote.

Each Living Thing
by Joanne Ryder
Harcourt 2000 (32p)
Poetic text asks readers to care for each living thing.

Nuts to You!
by Lois Ehlert
Harcourt 1993 (32p)
A frisky squirrel digs up bulbs, steals birdseed, and enters a house through a tear in a screen.

The Hatseller and the Monkeys
by Baba Wagué Diakité
Scholastic 1999 (32p)
A band of mischievous monkeys steals Bamusa's hats in an African version of a familiar tale.

The Bossy Gallito
by Lucía M. González
Scholastic 1999 (32p) paper
A bossy rooster learns a lesson about politeness. **Text in English and Spanish.**

Key

 Science

Social Studies

Multicultural

Music

Math

Classic

Art

---

* = Included in Houghton Mifflin Classroom Bookshelf, Level K

Books for Shared Reading

 Way Out in the Desert
by T. J. Marsh and J. Watson
Rising Moon (32p)
A song introduces readers
to the plants and animals
of the Sonoran Desert.

 Roar! A Noisy Counting Book
by Pamela Duncan Edwards
Harper 2000 (32p)
One lion cub and his nine
cubmates roar much too loudly
for their animal neighbors.

What Does the Rabbit Say?
by Jacque Hall
Bantam 2000
(32p)
A boy and girl
wonder what kind
of sound their pet
rabbit makes.

From Head to Toe
by Eric Carle
Harper 1997 (32p)
Children imitate animal movement.

 Little White Duck
by Walt Whipp
Little 2000 (32p)
A duck causes a commotion
on the pond in this song.

Do Pigs Have Stripes? *
by Melanie Walsh
Houghton 1996 (40p)
Bright pictures
illustrate a
series of silly
questions
about animals.
See others in
series.

Polar Bear, Polar Bear, What Do You Hear?
by Eric Carle
Holt 1991 (32p) also paper
Children learn about animal
sounds in this patterned story.

Books for Phonics Read Aloud

Bugs for Lunch
by Margery Facklam
Charlesbridge 1999 (32p)
Rhyming verse introduces
creatures that eat bugs.

Hug Bug
by Karen Hoenecke
School Zone 1997 (8p) paper
A girl's favorite bug is the one
that wears a silly hat.

Jamberry
by Bruce Degen
Harper 1983 (32p) also paper
A boy and a bear
share a berry
picking adventure.

* = Included in Houghton Mifflin Classroom Bookshelf, Level K

Technology

Computer Software Resources

- **Curious George® Learns Phonics**
- **Lexia Quick Phonics Assessment**
- **Lexia Phonics Intervention CD-ROM: Primary**
- **Published by Sunburst Technology** *
    Tenth Planet™ Vowels: Short and Long
    Curious George® Pre-K ABCs
    First Phonics
- **Published by The Learning Company**
    Dr. Seuss's ABC™
    Paint, Write, & Play!™
    ¡Vamos a Jugar, Pintar, y Escribir!
- **Animals Alike CD-ROM.** *Heinemann*

Video Cassettes

- **The Hat** *by Jan Brett. Spoken Arts*
- **The Little Red Hen** *by Paul Galdone. Weston Woods*
- **Move Like the Animals.** *Blackboard Entertainment*
- **Angus and the Ducks** *by Marjorie Flack. Weston Woods*
- **Will We Miss Them? Endangered Species** *by Alexandria Wright. Spoken Arts*

Audio Cassettes

- **The Three Little Pigs** *by Paul Galdone. Houghton*
- **Henny Penny** *by Paul Galdone. Spoken Arts*
- **Animal Groove.** *Blue Vision Music. Rounder Kids*
- **The Three Billy Goats Gruff** *by Paul Galdone. Houghton*
- **Annie and the Wild Animals** *by Jan Brett. Houghton*
- **Audiotapes for *A World of Animals.*** *Houghton Mifflin Company*

* © Sunburst Technology Corporation, a Houghton Mifflin Company.
   All Rights Reserved.
   Technology Resources addresses are on page R6.

Education Place
www.eduplace.com *Log on to* Education
Place *for more activities relating to* A World of
Animals.

Book Adventure
www.bookadventure.org *This Internet reading-
incentive program provides thousands of titles
for students to read.*

Theme 10

Theme at a Glance

Theme Concept: *Interesting animals are everywhere!*

 Indicates Tested Skills

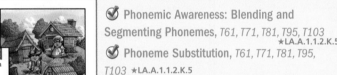

Learning to Read

	Phonemic Awareness and Phonics	High-Frequency Words	Comprehension Skills and Strategies
WEEK 1 **Read Aloud** **Run Away!** **Big Book** **Splash!** **Science Link** **Baby Animals Play** **Phonics Library** *"Ken and Jen"* 	☑ Phonemic Awareness: Blending and Segmenting Phonemes, *T9, T17, T27, T39, T47* ★LA.A.1.1.2.K.5 ☑ Phoneme Substitution, *T9, T17, T27, T39, T47* ★LA.A.1.1.2.K.5 ☑ Initial Consonant *j*, *T12–T13, T20–T21* ★LA.A.1.1.2.K.3, 5 ☑ Blending *-ug* words, *T34, T42–T43* ★LA.A.1.1.2.K.4, 5 **Phonics Review: Familiar Consonants; -ug, -et, -en words,** *T13, T36, T44, T50, T52* ★LA.A.1.1.2.K.3, 4, 5, 6	☑ High-Frequency Words, *T22–T23, T35, T51* ★LA.A.1.1.3.K.1 **Word Wall,** *T8, T16, T26, T38, T46* ★LA.A.1.1.3.K.1, 4	☑ Comprehension: Story Structure: Beginning, Middle, End, *T10, T18, T29, T30, T31, T48* ★LA.E.1.1.2.K.1 **Strategies: Question,** *T10, T18, T29, T40* LA.A.1.1.4.K.1 **Phonics/Decoding,** *T35* ★LA.A.1.1.2.K.3, 4, 5
WEEK 2 **Read Aloud** **The Tale of the Three Little Pigs** **Big Book** **Feathers for Lunch** **Science Link** **Which Pet?** **Phonics Library** *"It Can Fit"*	☑ Phonemic Awareness: Blending and Segmenting Phonemes, *T61, T71, T81, T95, T103* ★LA.A.1.1.2.K.5 ☑ Phoneme Substitution, *T61, T71, T81, T95, T103* ★LA.A.1.1.2.K.5 ☑ Reviewing Initial Consonants *b, c, l*, *T66–T67, T74–T75* ★LA.A.1.1.2.K.3, 5 ☑ Blending *-ut* words, *T90, T98–T99* ★LA.A.1.1.2.K.4, 5 **Phonics Review: Familiar Consonants; -ug, -ut, -en words,** *T67, T74, T92, T100, T106, T108* *LA.A.1.1.2.K.3, 4, 5, 6	☑ High-Frequency Words, *T76–T77, T91, T107* ★LA.A.1.1.3.K.1 **Word Wall,** *T60, T70, T80, T94, T102* ★LA.A.1.1.3.K.1, 4	☑ Comprehension: Compare and Contrast, *T62, T72, T83, T84, T85, T96, T104* FCAT Benchmark in Gr. 3–5 **Strategies: Predict/Infer,** *T62, T72, T83, T86, T96* LA.A.1.1.1.K.1 **Phonics/Decoding,** *T91* ★LA.A.1.1.2.K.3, 4, 5
WEEK 3 **Read Aloud** **Henny Penny** **Big Book** **Splash!** **Feathers for Lunch** **Science Links** **Baby Animals Play** **Which Pet?** **Phonics Library** *"The Bug Hut"* 	☑ Phonemic Awareness: Blending and Segmenting Phonemes, *T117, T127, T137, T145, T153* ★LA.A.1.1.2.K.4, 5 ☑ Phoneme Substitution, *T117, T127, T137, T145, T153* ★LA.A.1.1.2.K.5 ☑ Initial Consonants *d, j, n,* and *w, T122–T123, T130–T131* ★LA.A.1.1.2.K.3, 5 ☑ Blending *-ug* and *-ut* words, *T140, T148–T149* ★LA.A.1.1.2.K.4, 5 **Phonics Review: Familiar Consonants; -ug, -ut, -en words,** *T142, T150, T156, T158* *LA.A.1.1.2.K.3, 4, 5, 6	High-Frequency Words, *T132–T133, T141, T157* ★LA.A.1.1.3.K.1 **Word Wall,** *T116, T126, T136, T144, T152* ★LA.A.1.1.3.K.1, 4	☑ Comprehension: Story Structure: Plot, *T118, T128, T129, T138, T139, T154* ★LA.E.1.1.2.K.1 **Strategies: Summarize,** *T118, T128, T129, T138* LA.A.1.1.4.K.1 **Question,** *T146, T147* **Phonics/Decoding,** *T141* ★LA.A.1.1.2.K.3, 4, 5

Sunshine State Standards

LA.A = Reading
LA.B = Writing
LA.C = Listening/Viewing/Speaking

LA.D = Language
LA.E = Literature

★ = FCAT Benchmark in Gr. 3–5

 Half-Day Kindergarten
Focus on lessons for tested skills. ☑
Then choose other activities as time allows.

<table>
<tr><th colspan="2">Pacing</th><th colspan="2">Multi–age Classroom</th><th colspan="2">Technology</th></tr>
<tr><td colspan="2">• This theme is designed to take approximately 3 weeks, depending on your students' needs.</td><td colspan="2">**Related themes—**
• **Grade 1:** *Animal Adventures*</td><td colspan="2"> **Education Place: www.eduplace.com** Log on to Education Place for more activities relating to *A World of Animals*.
Florida Lesson Planner CD-ROM: Customize your planning for *A World of Animals* with the Florida Lesson Planner.</td></tr>
</table>

Word Work | Writing & Language | Centers

High-Frequency Word Practice	Building Words	Oral Language	Writing	Listening/ Speaking/Viewing	Content Areas
Matching Words, *T14* ★LA.A.1.1.3.K.1 Building Sentences, *T24* ★LA.A.1.1.3.K.1	Word Family -*ug*, *T36* ★LA.A.1.1.2.K.5 ★LA.A.1.1.3.K.4 Word Families -*ug*, -*et*, -*en*, *T44*, *T52* ★LA.A.1.1.2.K.5 ★LA.A.1.1.3.K.4	**Using Exact Naming Words** • animal names chart, *T15* ★LA.A.1.1.3.K.2 **Vocabulary Expansion** • comparing information, *T25* LA.C.1.1.4.K.1	**Shared Writing** • writing a report, *T37* **Interactive Writing** • writing a report, *T45* **Independent Writing** • Journals, *T53* LA.B.2.1.1.K.1 LA.C.2.1.1.K.1 LA.B.2.1.2.K.1 LA.B.1.1.3.K.2, 3 LA.B.2.1.1.K.1, 2 ★LA.A.1.1.3.K.1 LA.B.1.1.3.K.3	**Listening,** *T25* LA.C.1.1.4.K.1 **Viewing and Speaking,** *T37* LA.C.2.1.1.K.1 LA.C.3.1.3.K.1 **Listening, Speaking, and Viewing,** *T45* LA.C.1.1.4.K.1 LA.C.3.1.2.K.1 LA.C.2.1.1.K.1	**Book Center,** *T11* LA.A.2.1.2.K.1 **Phonics Center,** *T13, T21, T43* ★LA.A.1.1.2.K.2, 3, 5 **Writing Center,** *T15, T45* LA.B.2.1.2.K.1 **Science Center,** *T19, T33* SC.G.1.1.3 SC.F.1.1.5 **Dramatic Play Center,** *T25, T33* LA.C.3.1.1.K.1 LA.E.2.1.1.K.2
Matching Words, *T68* ★LA.A.1.1.3.K.1 Building Sentences, *T78* ★LA.A.1.1.3.K.1	Word Family -*ut*, *T92* ★LA.A.1.1.2.K.5 ★LA.A.1.1.3.K.4 Word Families -*ut*, -*ug*, -*et*, *T100* ★LA.A.1.1.2.K.5 ★LA.A.1.1.3.K.4 Word Families, *T108* ★LA.A.1.1.2.K.5 ★LA.A.1.1.3.K.4	**Using Rhyming Words** • rhyming chart, *T69* LA.D.2.1.2.K.1 **Vocabulary Expansion** • using exact words, rhyming words, *T79* ★LA.A.1.1.2.K.5 ★LA.A.1.1.3.K.2	**Shared Writing** • writing a book report, *T93* LA.E.2.1.1.K.2 LA.B.2.1.2.K.1 **Interactive Writing** • writing a book report, *T101* **Independent Writing** • Journals, *T109* LA.B.2.1.2.K.1 LA.E.2.1.1.K.2 LA.C.1.1.4.K.1 LA.B.2.1.2.K.1 ★LA.A.1.1.3.K.1 LA.E.2.1.1.K.1	**Listening and Viewing,** *T79* LA.C.2.1.1.K.1 LA.C.1.1.4.K.1 **Viewing and Speaking,** *T93* LA.C.2.1.1.K.1 LA.C.3.1.3.K.1 **Listening, Viewing, and Speaking,** *T101* LA.C.1.1.4.K.1 LA.C.2.1.1.K.1 LA.C.3.1.3.K.1	**Book Center,** *T58* LA.A.2.1.2.K.1 **Phonics Center,** *T67, T75, T99* ★LA.A.1.1.2.K.2, 3, 5 **Writing Center,** *T69, T101* **Dramatic Play Center,** *T63* TH.A.1.1.1 **Science Center,** *T73, T89* VA.A.1.1.1 SC.F.1.1.5 **Math Center,** *T89* SC.F.1.1.5 LA.D.2.1.2.K.1 LA.B.2.1.2.K.1 LA.A.2.1.2.K.1
Matching Words, *T124* ★LA.A.1.1.3.K.1 Building Sentences, *T134* ★LA.A.1.1.3.K.1	Word Families -*ug*, -*ut*, *T142* ★LA.A.1.1.2.K.5 ★LA.A.1.1.3.K.4 Word Families -*ug*, -*ut*, -*en*, *T150* ★LA.A.1.1.2.K.5 ★LA.A.1.1.3.K.4 Word Families -*ug*, -*ut*, -*en*, -*et*- *ot*, *T158* ★LA.A.1.1.2.K.5 ★LA.A.1.1.3.K.4	**Using Order Words** • order words chart, *T125* ★LA.E.1.1.2.K.1 **Vocabulary Expansion** • animal names, *T135* ★LA.A.1.1.3.K.3, 4	**Shared Writing** • writing directions, *T143* LA.B.1.1.2.K.1, 3 LA.C.1.1.1.K.1 **Interactive Writing** • writing directions, *T151* LA.B.1.1.2.K.1, 3 **Independent Writing** • Journals, *T159* LA.B.2.1.1.K.1	**Viewing,** *T135* LA.C.2.1.1.K.1 **Listening, Speaking, and Viewing,** *T143* LA.C.1.1.1.K.1 LA.C.2.1.1.K.1 LA.C.3.1.3.K.1 **Viewing and Speaking,** *T151* LA.C.2.1.1.K.1 LA.C.3.1.3.K.1	**Book Center,** *T129* LA.A.2.1.2.K.1 **Phonics Center,** *T123, T131, T149* ★LA.A.1.1.2.K.2, 3, 5 **Writing Center,** *T125, T151* **Science Center,** *T119* SC.D.1.1.3 **Math Center,** *T139* MA.C.1.1.1 LA.B.2.1.2.K.1 LA.E.2.1.1.K.2 LA.B.1.1.2.K.3

Planning for Assessment

Use these resources to meet your assessment needs. For additional information, see the *Teacher's Assessment Handbook.*

Emerging Literacy Survey

Lexia CD-ROM

Diagnostic Planning

Emerging Literacy Survey

- If you have used this survey to obtain baseline data on the skills children brought with them to kindergarten, this might be a good time to re-administer all or parts of the survey to chart progress, to identify areas of strength and need, and to test the need for early intervention.

Lexia Quick Phonics Assessment CD-ROM

- Can be used to identify students who need more help with phonics.

Ongoing Assessment

Phonemic Awareness:
- **Practice Book,** pp. 285–286, 295-296, 305–306

Phonics:
- **Practice Book,** pp. 287, 290, 291, 297, 300, 301, 307, 310, 311

Comprehension:
- **Practice Book** Reading Responses, pp. 283–284, 289, 293–294, 299, 303–304, 309

Writing:
- Writing samples for portfolios

Informal Assessment:
- **Diagnostic Checks,** pp. T23, T32, T43, T51, T77, T88, T99, T107, T133, T149, T157

Florida Integrated Theme Test

Theme Skills Test

End-of-Theme Assessment

Florida Integrated Theme Test:
- Assesses children's progress as readers and writers in a format that reflects instruction. Simple decodable texts test reading skills in context.

Theme Skills Test:
- Assesses children's mastery of specific reading and language arts skills taught in the theme.

Kindergarten Benchmarks

For your planning, listed here are the instructional goals and activities that help develop benchmark behaviors for kindergartners. Use this list to plan instruction and to monitor children's progress. See the Checklist of skills found on p. T161.

Theme Lessons and Activities:	Benchmark Behaviors:
Oral Language	
• songs, rhymes, chants	• can listen to a story attentively
• shared reading	• can participate in the shared reading experience
Phonemic Awareness	
• blending and segmenting phonemes	• can blend sounds into meaningful units
• substituting phonemes	
Phonics	
• initial consonants *b, c, d, j, l, w,*	• can name single letters and their sounds
• word families *-ug, ut*	• can decode some common CVC words
Concepts of Print	
• capital at beginning of sentence	
• end punctuation (period, question mark, exclamation mark)	• can recognize common print conventions
Reading	
• decodable texts	• can read and write a few words
• high-frequency words *are, he*	• can select a letter to represent a sound
Comprehension	
• fantasy/realism	• can think critically about a text
• noting details	• can use effective reading strategies
• drawing conclusions	
Writing and Language	
• drawing and labeling images	• can label pictures using phonetic spellings
• using exact naming words and order words	• can write independently
• journal writing	

LA.A.1.1.1.K.1
LA.C.2.1.1.K.1
LA.C.3.1.1.K.1

Launching the Theme

A World of Animals

Theme Poster: A World of Animals

Fun in the Sun: A Big Book of Florida

Big Book pages 20–21

▶ Using the Theme Poster

Tell children that in this theme they will learn about pets and about wild animals. Display the Theme Poster. *Which of these animals can you name? What do you know about them?*

- **Week 1** After reading *Run Away!*, discuss other favorite animal stories. *Are the animals real or make-believe? Do they tell us anything about people?*
- **Week 2** The animals in *Splash!* live in a hot, dry place. Discuss the animals on the Poster, where they live, and how they are suited to their locales.
- **Week 3** Use *Feathers for Lunch* to inspire young birdwatchers! Have children compare the birds in the book to the toucan on the Poster. As bird-watchers, children can look for birds outdoors and record their special features in their journals.

Multi-age Classroom

Related theme

Grade 1 . . . Animal Adventures

▲

Grade K . . . A World of Animals

Sunshine State Standards pp. xii–xiii

★ = FCAT Benchmark in Gr. 3–5

★**LA.A.1.1.3.K.3** sorts words from categories	**LA.A.2.1.5.K.2** pictures, signs for information
LA.A.1.1.1.K.1 oral predictions	**LA.B.2.1.3.K.1** uses computer for writing

▶ Theme Poem: "Giraffes Don't Huff"

Read the poem "Giraffes Don't Huff," exaggerating the words that describe animal sounds (*huff, hoot, howl, growl, roar*) and making your voice very quiet at the end. Children love imitating animal sounds, so recite the poem a few times and invite them to join in.

On-Going Project

LA.A.2.1.5.K.2
★LA.A.1.1.3.K.3

> Materials • toy animals • animal masks • animal books and videos • objects with decorative animal motifs

The Class Zoo Display the Theme Poster as a background for a Class Zoo. Children can add their own drawings of interesting animals of all kinds.

- Children can bring in toy animals or search through old magazines for pictures. They can make a label for each one telling its name, where it lives, and other information about it.
- Share picture books or show a video about animals. Children who are interested in special animals can ask their parents or the librarian to help them learn more.
- Children might bring photos of their pets to school. They can write about their pets or write directions for their care. Children can take turns being the "zookeeper," telling classmates or visitors about the Class Zoo.

Challenge Children can count all the animals, categorize them in various ways (pets vs. wild animals, real vs. make-believe animals, and so on), and report to the class on how many of each kind are in the display.

The Class Z**oo**

dogs	10
cats	12
cows	2
tigers	3
snakes	2

Giraffes Don't Huff

Giraffes don't huff or hoot or howl
They never grump, they never growl
They never roar, they never riot,
They eat green leaves
And just keep quiet.

by Karla Kuskin

Higglety Pigglety: A Book of Rhymes, *page 42*

 *Technology*

LA.B.2.1.3.K.1

www.eduplace.com
Log onto *Education Place* for more activities relating to *A World of Animals.*

 Florida Lesson Planner CD-ROM
Customize your planning for *A World of Animals* with the Florida Lesson Planner.

Book Adventure
www.bookadventure.org
This Internet reading-incentive program provides thousands of titles for students to read.

 Home Connection

Send home the theme news letter for *A World of Animals* to introduce the theme and suggest home activities (Blackline Master 141).

 For other suggestions relating to *A World of Animals*, see **Home/Community Connections.**

Theme 10

Classroom Routines

A World of Animals

To introduce a routine...

1 Demonstrate the routine for the class.

2 Cycle every child through the routine at least once with supervision.

3 Establish ground rules for acceptable work products.

4 Check children's work.

5 Praise children's growing independence.

Instructional Routines

Substituting Phonemes

By now many children will enjoy the challenge of substituting phonemes. Make these oral activities fun.

Create funny nonsense variations of familiar nursery rhymes with playful phoneme substitutions, for example, "Zinkle, zinkle, little star" or "Mack and Mill went up the hill." Children give the right words and then suggest funny phoneme substitutions of their own.

Play Pass the Word by giving children a simple word and having them change the first or last phoneme before passing it to the next person. For example *fan* becomes *fat*, then *cat*, then *can*, and so on.

Independent Writing

Through Shared and Interactive Writing, children develop more independence in writing. By now some children may even be able to write a couple of sentences or a whole "story" in their journals. Provide time for daily journal writing.

Have children decorate covers for their own Summer Journals. With parents' encouragement and help, children can keep a journal of their summer experiences to share with their teacher and classmates in the fall when they begin the new school year.

Management Routines

The Year in Review

The end of the kindergarten year is a good time to recognize children's accomplishments. During the last theme, provide time for children to review their portfolios, writing samples, and journals to see how much they've learned about letters, words, and sentences. Also compare these samples of children's early work and recent work with parents at year-end conferences.

NOTE: Some teachers like to gather examples of children's best work and place them in a notebook. At the end of the year, the notebook can be passed on to the first grade teacher.

Teacher's Note

By now children will be following familiar routines with ease. Get them to suggest solutions for any new problems that arise. Ask, for example, how *they* could help figure out whether there are enough letter cards for an activity or help make sure everyone has a handout at dismissal time.

Literature for Week 1
Different texts for different purposes

Teacher Read Aloud

RUN AWAY!
■ based on a Kootenai Tale ■
by Gerald McDermott

Purposes

- oral language
- listening strategy
- comprehension skill

Big Books:

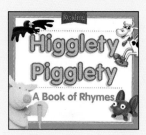

Higglety Pigglety: A Book of Rhymes

Purposes

- oral language development
- phonemic awareness

From Apples to Zebras: A Book of ABC's

Purposes

- alphabet recognition
- letters and sounds

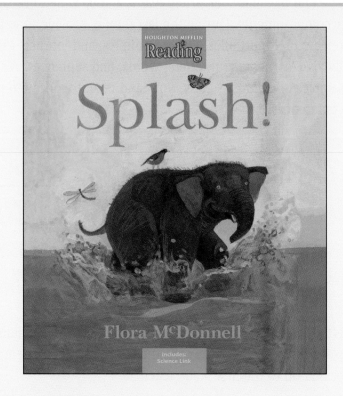

Splash!
Flora McDonnell
Includes: Science Link

Big Book: Main Selection

Purposes

- concepts of print
- reading strategy
- story language
- comprehension skills

Also available in Little Big Book and audiotape

Leveled Books

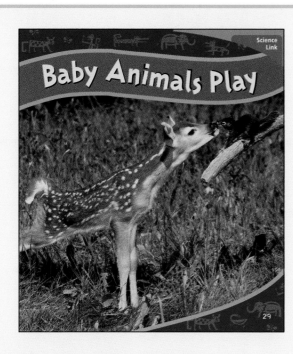

Also in the Big Book:
– Science Link

Purposes

- reading strategies
- comprehension skills
- concepts of print

Phonics Library

Also available
in Take-Home
version

Purposes

- applying phonics skills and
high-frequency words

On My Way Paperback

Animals at Play

by Wil Perry
page T155

Little Readers for
Guided Reading
Collection K

Houghton Mifflin
Classroom Bookshelf
Level K

www.eduplace.com

Log on to *Education Place* for more activities
relating to *A World of Animals.*

www.bookadventure.org

This free Internet reading-incentive program
provides thousands of titles for students to read.

Suggested Daily Routines

Instructional Goals

Learning to Read

✓ *Phonemic Awareness:* Blending and Segmenting Phonemes, Phoneme Substitution

Strategy Focus: Question

✓ *Comprehension Skill:* Story Structure: Beginning, Middle, End

✓ *Phonics Skills*

Phonemic Awareness: Beginning Sound /j/

Initial Consonant *J, j*

Compare and Review: Initial Consonants: *r, z*

✓ *High-Frequency Word: are*

✓ *Concepts of Print:* Capital at the Beginning of a Sentence

Word Work

High-Frequency Word Practice: Word Families: *-ug, -et, -en*

Writing & Language

Vocabulary Skill: Using Exact Naming Words, Comparing Information

Writing Skills: Writing a Report

Sunshine State Standards Achieved Each Day

LA.A = Reading
LA.B = Writing
LA.C = Listening/Viewing/Speaking
LA.D = Language
LA.E = Literature

★ = FCAT Benchmark in Grades 3–5

Day 1

Opening Routines, *T8–T9*   LA.A.2.1.5.K.2
★LA.A.1.1.2.K.5, 6
★LA.A.1.1.3.K.4

Word Wall
- Phonemic Awareness: Blending and Segmenting Phonemes, Phoneme Substitution

Teacher Read Aloud
Run Away!, T10–T11   LA.C.1.1.1.K.2
- **Strategy:** Question   LA.A.1.1.4.K.1
- **Comprehension:** Story Structure: Beginning, Middle, End   ★LA.E.1.1.2.K.1

Phonics
Instruction
- Phonemic Awareness, Beginning Sound /j/, *T12–T13; Practice Book, 285–286*   ★LA.A.1.1.2.K.2, 3, 5

High-Frequency Word Practice
- Words: *I, go, to, see, a, the, T14*   ★LA.A.1.1.3.K.1

Oral Language
- Using Exact Naming Words, *T15*   ★LA.A.1.1.3.K.4

★ LA.A.1.1.2.K.2 knows alphabet
★ LA.A.1.1.2.K.3 knows sounds of alphabet
★ LA.A.1.1.2.K.5 basic phonetic principles
★ LA.A.1.1.2.K.6 print conveys meaning
★ LA.A.1.1.3.K.1 identifies high frequency words
★ LA.A.1.1.3.K.2 identifies noun words
★ LA.A.1.1.3.K.4 uses sources to build vocabulary
★ LA.E.1.1.2.K.1 sequence of events, setting
   LA.A.1.1.4.K.1 strategies to comprehend text
   LA.A.2.1.5.K.2 pictures, signs for information
   LA.C.1.1.1.K.2 listens to oral language

Day 2

Opening Routines, *T16–T17*   LA.A.2.1.5.K.2
★LA.A.1.1.2.K.5, 6
★LA.A.1.1.3.K.4

Word Wall
- Phonemic Awareness: Blending and Segmenting Phonemes, Phoneme Substitution

Sharing the Big Book
Splash!, T18–T19   LA.C.1.1.1.K.1
- **Strategy:** Question   LA.A.1.1.4.K.1
- **Comprehension:** Story Structure: Beginning, Middle, End   ★LA.E.1.1.2.K.1

Phonics
Instruction, Practice
- Initial Consonant *j, T20–T21*   ★LA.A.1.1.2.K.3, 5
- *Practice Book, 287*

High-Frequency Word
- New Word: *are, T22–T23*   ★LA.A.1.1.3.K.1
- *Practice Book, 288*

High-Frequency Word Practice
- Words: *A, a, and, at, for, are, the, T24*   ★LA.A.1.1.3.K.1

Vocabulary Expansion
- Comparing Information, *T25*   LA.C.1.1.4.K.1

★ LA.A.1.1.2.K.3 knows sounds of alphabet
★ LA.A.1.1.2.K.5 basic phonetic principles
★ LA.A.1.1.2.K.6 print conveys meaning
★ LA.A.1.1.3.K.1 identifies high frequency words
★ LA.A.1.1.3.K.4 uses sources to build vocabulary
★ LA.E.1.1.2.K.1 sequence of events, setting
   LA.A.1.1.4.K.1 strategies to comprehend text
   LA.A.2.1.5.K.2 pictures, signs for information
   LA.C.1.1.1.K.1 follows 2-step oral directions
   LA.C.1.1.4.K.1 listens for specific information

✓ = tested skills

Leveled Books, p. T49   LA.A.2.1.2.K.1

Half-Day Kindergarten
Focus on lessons for tested skills. ✓
Then choose other activities as time allows.

Technology
Florida Lesson Planner CD-ROM
Customize your planning for *the week*
with the Florida Lesson Planner.

Key correlations are provided in
this chart. Additional correlations
are provided at point of use.

Day 3

Opening Routines, *T26–T27*   LA.A.2.1.5.K.2
★ LA.A.1.1.2.K.5, 6
★ LA.A.1.1.3.K.4
Word Wall
• **Phonemic Awareness:** Blending and
Segmenting Phonemes, Phoneme
Substitution

Sharing the Big Book   LA.C.1.1.1.K.2
Splash!, *T28–T31*   LA.A.1.1.4.K.1
• **Strategy:** Question   LA.A.1.1.4.K.1
★ LA.E.1.1.2.K.1
• **Comprehension:** Story Structure: Beginning,
Middle, End, *T29; Practice Book, 289*
• **Concepts of Print:** Capital at the Beginning of
a Sentence, *T31*   ★ LA.A.1.1.2.K.4

Phonics
Practice, Application
• Consonant *j, T34–T35*   ★ LA.A.1.1.2.K.3, 5

Instruction   ★ LA.A.1.1.2.K.5
• Blending *j -ug, T34–T35; Practice Book, 290*
• Phonics Library: "Ken and Jen," *T35*
★ LA.A.1.1.2.K.5

Building Words
• Word Family: *-ug, T36*   ★ LA.A.1.1.2.K.5
★ LA.A.1.1.3.K.4

Shared Writing
LA.B.2.1.2.K.1
• Writing a Report, *T37*   LA.B.1.1.3.K.2, 3
• Viewing and Speaking, *T37*   LA.C.2.1.1.K.1
LA.C.3.1.3.K.1

Day 4

Opening Routines, *T38–T39*   LA.A.2.1.5.K.2
★ LA.A.1.1.2.K.5, 6
★ LA.A.1.1.3.K.4
Word Wall
• **Phonemic Awareness:** Blending and
Segmenting Phonemes, Phoneme
Substitution   ★ LA.A.1.1.2.K.2, 3, 5

Sharing the Big Book   ★ LA.A.2.1.1.K.1
Science Link: "Baby Animals Play," *T40–T41*
• **Strategy:** Question   LA.A.1.1.4.K.1
• **Comprehension:** Story Structure: Beginning,
Middle, End
• **Concepts of Print:** Capital at the Beginning
of a Sentence   ★ LA.A.1.1.2.K.4

Phonics
Practice
• Blending *-ug* Words, *T42–T43; Practice Book,*
291   ★ LA.A.1.1.2.K.5

Building Words
• Word Families: *-ug, -et, -en, T44*   ★ LA.A.1.1.2.K.5
★ LA.A.1.1.3.K.4

Interactive Writing
• Writing a Report, *T45*   LA.B.2.1.1.K.1, 2
★ LA.A.1.1.3.K.1
LA.B.1.1.3.K.3

Day 5

Opening Routines, *T46–T47*   LA.A.2.1.5.K.2
★ LA.A.1.1.2.K.5, 6
★ LA.A.1.1.3.K.4
Word Wall
• **Phonemic Awareness:** Blending and
Segmenting Phonemes, Phoneme
Substitution   ★ LA.A.1.1.2.K.2, 3, 5

Revisiting the Literature
Comprehension: Story Structure: Beginning,
Middle, End, *T48*   ★ LA.E.1.1.2.K.1

Building Fluency
• Phonics Library: "Ken and Jen," *T49*
LA.A.1.1.4.K.1
★ LA.A.1.1.2.K.5
Phonics
Review
• Consonants, Word Families *T50*   ★ LA.A.1.1.2.K.5
★ LA.A.1.1.3.K.4

High-Frequency Word Review
• Words, *I, see, my, like, a, to, and, go, is, here,*
for, have, said, are, the, She, play, T51;
Practice Book, 292   ★ LA.A.1.1.3.K.1

Building Words
• Word Families: *-et, -en, -ug, T52*   ★ LA.A.1.1.2.K.5
★ LA.A.1.1.3.K.4

Independent Writing
• Journals: Naming Animals, *T53*   LA.B.2.1.1.K.1

★ **LA.A.1.1.2.K.3** knows sounds of alphabet
★ **LA.A.1.1.2.K.4** concept of words, meaning
★ **LA.A.1.1.2.K.5** basic phonetic principles
★ **LA.A.1.1.2.K.6** print conveys meaning
★ **LA.A.1.1.3.K.4** uses sources to build vocabulary
★ **LA.E.1.1.2.K.1** sequence of events, setting
LA.A.1.1.4.K.1 strategies to comprehend text
LA.A.2.1.5.K.2 pictures, signs for information
LA.B.1.1.3.K.2 directionality of print
LA.B.1.1.3.K.3 uses end punctuation
LA.B.2.1.2.K.1 writes with pictures, words
LA.C.1.1.1.K.2 listens to oral language
LA.C.2.1.1.K.1 main idea in nonprint
LA.C.3.1.3.K.1 uses speaking vocabulary

★ **LA.A.1.1.2.K.2** knows alphabet
★ **LA.A.1.1.2.K.3** knows sounds of alphabet
★ **LA.A.1.1.2.K.4** concept of words, meaning
★ **LA.A.1.1.2.K.5** basic phonetic principles
★ **LA.A.1.1.2.K.6** print conveys meaning
★ **LA.A.1.1.3.K.1** identifies high frequency words
★ **LA.A.1.1.3.K.4** uses sources to build vocabulary
★ **LA.A.2.1.1.K.1** main idea from a read-aloud
LA.A.1.1.4.K.1 strategies to comprehend text
LA.A.2.1.5.K.2 pictures, signs for information
LA.B.1.1.3.K.3 uses end punctuation
LA.B.2.1.1.K.1 uses pictures, words
LA.B.2.1.1.K.2 ideas to shared writing

★ **LA.A.1.1.2.K.2** knows alphabet
★ **LA.A.1.1.2.K.3** knows sounds of alphabet
★ **LA.A.1.1.2.K.5** basic phonetic principles
★ **LA.A.1.1.2.K.6** print conveys meaning
★ **LA.A.1.1.3.K.1** identifies high frequency words
★ **LA.A.1.1.3.K.4** uses sources to build vocabulary
★ **LA.E.1.1.2.K.1** sequence of events, setting
LA.A.1.1.4.K.1 strategies to comprehend text
LA.A.2.1.5.K.2 pictures, signs for information
LA.B.2.1.1.K.1 uses pictures, words

 Independent Writing Activity, p. T53   LA.B.2.1.1.K.1

Setting up the Centers

Management Tip Ask children for *their* ideas for topics to explore in the Centers. What do they want to learn about? What animals from this theme's stories interest them most? What favorite activities would they like to repeat during this theme? Use children's ideas to supplement the Centers outlined here.

★LA.A.1.1.2.K.2, 3, 5

Phonics Center

Materials • Phonics Center materials for Theme 10, Week 1

This week children sort pictures whose names begin with / j /, / r /, or / z /. They make words with the letters *b, h, r,* and the word family *-ug,* and they also build sentences with Word Cards.

Prepare materials for Days 1, 2, and 4. Cut apart the letter grids and put them in plastic bags by color. Put out the Workmats and open the Direction Chart to the appropriate day. See pages T13, T21, and T43 for this week's Phonics Center activities.

LA.A.2.1.2.K.1

Book Center

Materials • books about animals around the world

In addition to the animal books listed in the Bibliography, put some old favorites in the Book Center after reading them aloud. See page T11 for this week's Book Center idea.

Animal ABC's by the World Wildlife Fund

Blueberries for Sal by Robert McCloskey

Hot Hippo by Mwenye Hadithi

What Does the Rabbit Say? by Jacque Hall

Sunshine State Standards pp. T6–T7   ★ = FCAT Benchmark in Gr. 3–5

★LA.A.1.1.2.K.2 knows alphabet   ★LA.A.1.1.2.K.5 basic phonetic principles
★LA.A.1.1.2.K.3 knows sounds of alphabet   LA.A.2.1.2.K.1 reads for pleasure

Writing Center

LA.B.1.1.2.K.4

Materials • crayons, markers • lined and unlined writing paper

This week children copy and illustrate a sentence about seeing a woodland animal. Later they illustrate the class report and write or dictate captions. See pages T15 and T45 for the Writing Center activities.

Animals in the Woods

fox   raccoon

bear   squirrel

rabbit

I go to the

to see a _____.

Science Center

SC.G.1.1.3

Materials • Blackline Masters 147–148 • word cards for *hot* and *cold* • chart paper • crayons or markers

Children sort animals according to climate (hot or cold). They also complete a comparison chart of animal features and talk about them. See pages T19 and T33 for Science Center activities.

hot   cold

Art Center

VA.A.1.1.1

Materials • Blackline Masters 149–150 • audiotape of loud/ soft everyday sounds

Children cut out the pictures on **Blackline Masters 149–150**, listen to the audiotape, and pantomime the sounds, and categorize the pictures. Children also dramatize the story *Splash!* See pages T25 and T33 for this week's Dramatic Play Center activities.

Learning to Read

Day 1

Day at a Glance

Learning to Read

Read Aloud:

Run Away!

☑ **Learning About /j/,** *page T12*

Word Work

☑ **High-Frequency Word Practice,** *page T14*

Writing & Language

Oral Language, *page T15*

Managing Small Groups

Teacher-Led Group
- Begin *Practice Book,* 283–286.
- Reread familiar **Phonics Library** selections.

Independent Groups
- Finish *Practice Book,* 283–286.
- Phonics Center: Theme 10, Week 1, Day 1
- Book, Writing, other Centers

Opening

LA.A.2.1.5.K.2
★LA.A.1.1.2.K.6
★LA.A.1.1.3.K.4

Calendar

Sunday	Monday	Tuesday	Wednesday	Thursday	Friday	Saturday
			1	2	3	4
5	6	7	8	9	10	11
12	13	14	15	16	17	18
19	20	21	22	23	24	25
26	27	28	29	30	31	

Chant the days of the week several times with children, pointing to each day as you chant its name. Ask children to jump when you come to today's name.

Daily Message

Interactive Writing Share the pen and coach children to help write today's message. Have volunteers write their names or the first letter in each word, for example. Remind children to use a capital letter for the beginning of a sentence or a name.

Karen, Mark, Keith, and Chris have cats. Gary, Russell, Pat, and Joyce have dogs.

Play "Pass the Pointer." Name a word and pass the pointer to a child. That child finds the word on the Word Wall, reads it, and passes the pointer to another child who finds and reads the next word you say.

★LA.A.1.2.K.5
LA.C.1.1.4.K.1

 Daily Phonemic Awareness
Blending and Segmenting Phonemes

Read "Jack and Jill" on page 43 of *Higglety Pigglety*. Then play a blending game.

- *I'll say some sounds. You put them together to make a word from the poem: /j/...
/a/... /ck/ (Jack). Now it's your turn to say each sound. Listen as I say the word slowly.*
Say *Jack,* stretching out the sounds. *What is the first sound? (/j/) the middle sound?*
(/ă/) the end sound? (/k/)

- Continue, having children blend and then segment the sounds in *came* and *pail*.

 Phoneme Substitution

This time we're going to change one sound to make a new word. Listen:
Jack. If we take away /j/, what is left? (/ack/) Now add /b/ to /ack/. What
new word do we get? (back) Continue, having children substitute /n/ for
/k/ in *came* to get *name*; then substitute /n/ for /p/ in *pail* to get *nail.*

Sunshine State Standards pp. T8–T9
★ = FCAT Benchmark in Gr. 3–5

★**LA.A.1.1.2.K.5** basic phonetic principles
★**LA.A.1.1.2.K.6** print conveys meaning
★**LA.A.1.1.3.K.4** uses sources to build vocabulary
LA.A.2.1.5.K.2 pictures, signs for information
LA.C.1.1.4.K.1 listens for specific information

Getting Ready to Learn

To help plan their day, tell children that they will

- listen to a book called
Run Away!

- meet a new Alphafriend.

- read more about animals in
the Book Center.

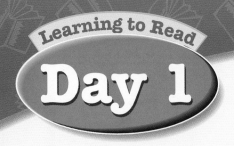

Read Aloud

RUN AWAY!
· based on a Kootenai Tale ·

by Gerald McDermott

Purposes • oral language • listening strategy • comprehension skill

Selection Summary
A coyote, a wolf, and a bear learn a lesson about following another's lead without knowing the reasons.

Key Concepts
Woodland animals
Stories that tell why

MEETING INDIVIDUAL NEEDS

English Language Learners

★LA.A.1.1.3.K.4

English language learners may be unfamiliar with many of the story words. Before reading, teach ways of moving: *scampering, running, dashed, disappeared, sped, chasing, jumped up, raced.* Then teach ways of talking: *gasped* and *shouted.*

LA.C.1.1.1.K.2
LA.A.1.1.1.K.1
LA.C.1.1.1.K.2
LA.A.1.1.4.K.1
★LA.E.1.1.2.K.1

Teacher Read Aloud
Oral Language/Comprehension

▶ **Building Background**

Display the cover and read the author's name. Tell children that in this book they will hear about some wild animals that live in the woods. Talk about types of woodland animals, including the wolf and coyote shown on the first page.

The note on the copyright page gives the origin of the tale. Explain that this is one of many stories made up to tell why animals behave as they do.

Strategy: Question

Teacher Modeling Read the title and share a few illustrations. Then model how to pose questions you think the text will answer.

Think Aloud

Asking myself questions as I read makes a story even more interesting. Let's see ... The title says Run Away! *That makes me ask this: Who runs away? What are they running away from? Let's look for the answers as we read.*

✓ **Comprehension Focus:**
Story Structure: Beginning, Middle, End

Teacher Modeling Tell children that remembering when things happen in a story helps readers retell it. Page through the book, asking children to notice what the animals are doing at the beginning and in the middle of the story.

Think Aloud

• *I see the rabbit is running at the beginning of the story. The beginning is usually where we see what the characters' problem is.*

• *In the middle of the story, other animals seem to be following the rabbit.*

• *I wonder what will happen at the end. Will we see how the problem is solved? Let's read and find out.*

Sunshine State Standards pp. T10–T11   ★ = FCAT Benchmark in Gr. 3–5

★LA.A.1.1.3.K.4 uses sources to build vocabulary   LA.A.1.1.4.K.1 strategies to comprehend text
★LA.E.1.1.2.K.1 sequence of events, setting   LA.A.2.1.2.K.1 reads for pleasure
LA.A.1.1.1.K.1 oral predictions   LA.C.1.1.1.K.2 listens to oral language

▶ Listening to the Story

This story uses vivid action words to tell how the animals move. Read aloud with expression, and allow time at each page for children to picture the action. Read slowly when the animals are resting and slightly faster when they are rushing.

▶ Responding

Retelling the Story Help children retell parts of the story.

■ *What happened at the beginning of the story? What was Little Rabbit's problem?*

■ *What three animals followed Little Rabbit in the middle of the story? Why?*

■ *What did Coyote, Wolf, and Bear find out at the end of the story?*

■ *Nowadays what does Little Rabbit do when he hears wind in the trees? What do the others do?*

Practice Book pages 283–284 Children will complete the pages during small group time.

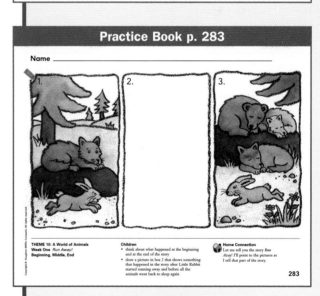

Practice Book p. 284

Practice Book p. 283

At Group Time

LA.A.2.1.2.K.1

Book Center

Children will have fun learning about animals around the world. Keep your "book zoo" stocked with titles like *Do Pigs Have Stripes?* by Melanie Walsh, *Animal ABC's* by the World Wildlife Fund, *Hot Hippo* by Mwenye Hadithi, *What Does the Rabbit Say?* by Jacque Hall, *Good-Night, Owl* by Pat Hutchins, *Northwest Animal Babies* by Art Wolfe and Andrea Helman, and *Blueberries for Sal* by Robert McCloskey.

Teacher's Note

Begin a chart of animals that live in a forest. Children can post pictures from magazines or their own illustrations next to each animal's name. During the theme, make similar charts for animals from other habitats. Use pictures from **Theme Posters** and any animal lotto game to spark ideas.

Phonemic Awareness

✓ Beginning Sound

▶ Introducing the Alphafriend: Jumping Jill

Use the Alphafriend routine to introduce Jumping Jill.

① Alphafriend Riddle Read these clues:

- *This Alphafriend's sound is /j/. Say it with me: /j/.*

- *This time the friend is a person who likes to play with something. See if you can guess what she plays with.*

- *This thing is long and thin, and it has handles. The girl uses it to join in jumping games.*

- *She jumps for joy as she swings this item over her head and under her feet. What is it?*

When most hands are up, call on children until they guess *jump rope.*

② Pocket Chart Display Jumping Jill in the pocket chart. Say her name, exaggerating the /j/ sound slightly, and have children echo.

③ **Alphafriend Audiotape** Play Jumping Jill's song. *Listen for words that start with /j/.*

④ Alphafolder Have children look at the scene and name all the /j/ pictures.

⑤ Summarize

- *What is our Alphafriend's name? What is her sound?*

- *What words in our Alphafriend's song start with /j/?*

- *Each time you look at Jumping Jill this week, remember the /j/ sound.*

Home Connection

A take-home version of Jumping Jill's song is on an **Alphafriends Blackline Master.** Children can share the song with their families.

MEETING INDIVIDUAL NEEDS
English Language Learners

★LA.A.1.1.2.K.3
In many languages, such as Spanish, the /j/ sound does not exist. English language learners often pronounce /j/ as /sh/ or /y/. Explain the position of the tongue, and provide mirrors for children to look at their mouths when practicing. Suggest that they remember a favorite word for the /j/ sound, such as *jump*.

Jumping Jill
(Tune: "Twinkle, Twinkle, Little Star")

Jumping Jill can jump
  so high.
Jill can jump in warm July.
Jumping Jill can jump
  so low.
Jill can jump for joy,
  you know.
Join her in a jumping game.
As you jump, call out her name!

Sunshine State Standards pp. T12–T13   ★ = FCAT Benchmark in Gr. 3–5

★**LA.A.1.1.2.K.2** knows alphabet
★**LA.A.1.1.2.K.3** knows sounds of alphabet
★**LA.A.1.1.2.K.5** basic phonetic principles

▶ Listening for /j/

Compare and Review: /r/, /z/ Display Alphafriends *Reggie Rooster* and *Zelda Zebra* opposite *Jumping Jill*. Review each character's sound.

Tell children you'll name some pictures and they should signal "thumbs up" for each one that begins like Jumping Jill's name. Volunteers put those cards below Jill's picture. For "thumbs down" words, volunteers put cards below the correct Alphafriends. Pictures: *jam, jar, jeep, jug, rake, rock, rug, zigzag, zip, zipper.*

▶ Apply

Practice Book pages 285–286 Children will complete the pages at small group time.

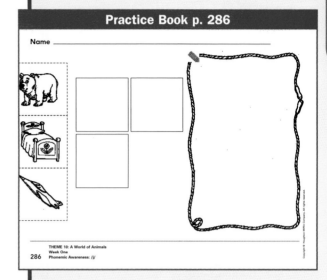

Practice Book p. 286

Name

THEME 10: A World of Animals
Week One
286 Phonemic Awareness: /j/

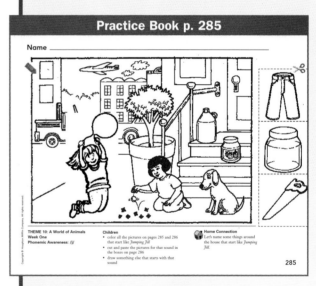

Practice Book p. 285

Name

THEME 10: A World of Animals
Week One
Phonemic Awareness: /j/

Children
- color all the pictures on pages 285 and 286 that start like *Jumping Jill*
- cut and paste the pictures for that sound in the boxes on page 286
- draw something else that starts with that sound

Home Connection
Let's name some things around the house that start like *Jumping Jill*.

285

At Group Time

Phonics Center

★LA.A.1.1.2.K.2, 3, 5

Use the Phonics Center materials for **Theme 10, Week 1, Day 1**.

Phonemic Awareness (T13)

★LA.A.1.1.3.K.1
LA.B.1.1.1.K.1
LA.B.2.1.2.K.1

High-Frequency Word Practice

▶ Matching Words

■ Display the high-frequency Word Cards *I, go, to, see, a, the* in a pocket chart. Call on children to identify each word and match it on the Word Wall.

■ Distribute the Word Cards. Then read the poem "One, Two, Three, Four, Five," one line at a time. Pause for children to match their cards to the same words in the poem. Then ask which Word Card did not have a match. (*to*) Redistribute the cards and continue until everyone has a turn.

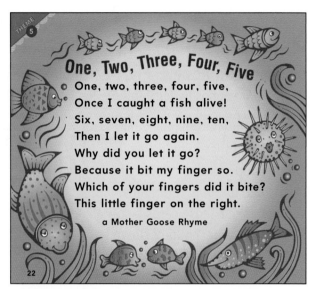

Higglety Pigglety: A Book of Rhymes, page 22

OBJECTIVES

Children
- read high-frequency words
- create and write sentences with high-frequency words

MATERIALS

- **Word Cards** *a, I, go, see, the, to*
- **Picture Card** *zoo*
- ***Higglety Pigglety: A Book of Rhymes,*** page 22
- **Punctuation Card:** period

✏ **Writing Opportunity** Review the word *at*, and add it to the Word Cards from the activity above along with the Picture Card *zoo*. Have small groups take turns using the cards to make a sentence as shown. Each group can brainstorm a list of animals to complete the sentence and make a picture card for one they choose. Later, children can write the sentence on paper and add their own drawings to complete it.

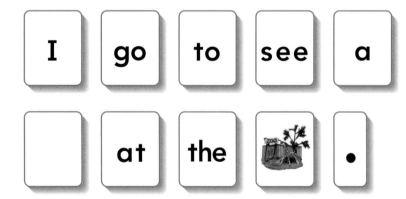

Sunshine State Standards pp. T14–T15   ★ = FCAT Benchmark in Gr. 3–5

★**LA.A.1.1.3.K.1** identifies high frequency words   **LA.B.1.1.1.K.1** uses prewriting strategies
★**LA.A.1.1.3.K.2** identifies noun words   **LA.B.2.1.2.K.1** writes with pictures, words

Oral Language

▶ Using Exact Naming Words

■ Guide children in pantomiming a walk through the woods. Pause to "see" the animals from *Run Away!*

■ Next, write *Animals in the Woods* on chart paper. Explain that *animals* is a general word, one that could mean *any* animals.

■ Ask children to name specific animals that they might see in the woods. List ideas on the chart. Reread the list, adding a quick sketch of each animal if possible. Explain that all the words on the list are *exact* naming words because they name a single kind of animal.

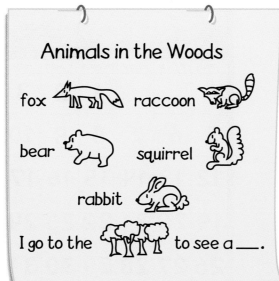

Animals in the Woods

fox   raccoon

bear   squirrel

rabbit

I go to the 🌳🌳🌳 to see a ___.

■ Write *I go to the woods to see a _____*. Help children read the sentence. Then invite them to complete it with one of the animal names on the chart.

At Group Time

Writing Center

LA.B.2.1.2.K.1

Put the chart in the Writing Center. Partners can read the sentence and complete it with their favorite animal name or a picture on an index card. Some children will be able to copy and illustrate their sentences.

I go to the
to see a bunny.

Day at a Glance

Learning to Read

Big Book:

Splash!

✓ **Phonics: Initial Consonant *j*,** *page T20*

✓ **High-Frequency Word *are*,** *page T22*

Word Work

High-Frequency Word Practice, *page T24*

Writing & Language

Vocabulary Expansion, *page T25*

Managing Small Groups

Teacher-Led Group
● Begin *Practice Book,* 287–288 and handwriting **Blackline Masters 166 or 192.**

Independent Groups
● Finish *Practice Book,* 287–288 and handwriting **Blackline Masters 166 or 192.**
● **Phonics Center:** Theme 10, Week 1, Day 2
● Science, Dramatic Play, other Centers

Opening

LA.A.2.1.5.K.2
★LA.A.1.1.2.K.6
★LA.A.1.1.3.K.4

Calendar

Sunday	Monday	Tuesday	Wednesday	Thursday	Friday	Saturday
			1	2	3	4
5	6	7	8	9	10	11
12	13	14	15	16	17	18
19	20	21	22	23	24	25
26	27	28	29	30	31	

Have children name the months of the year with you. As you chant the months again, have children jump for each one that begins with the /j/ sound.

Daily Message

Interactive Writing Children can help you write a message for the animals in *Run Away!* Ask children what they think the animals learned from chasing Little Rabbit. You might explain the old saying "Look before you leap."

Dear Coyote, Wolf, and Bear,

Next time ask Little Rabbit why he is afraid.

Have children chant the spelling of each word on the wall today: **P-l-a-y** *spells* play; s-e-e *spells* see; m-y *spells* my; l-i-k-e *spells* like.

Routines

 ## Daily Phonemic Awareness
Blending and Segmenting Phonemes

Display Picture Cards *hen, pig, dog, cat,* and *goat.* Then play a blending game.

- *I'll say some sounds. You put them together to name one of the animals.*
  Listen: / h / / ĕ / / n /. *(hen)*

- *Now it's your turn to say each sound.* Say *hen* slowly, stretching out the sounds.
  What is the first sound in hen? (/h/) *Listen again:* hen. *What is the middle sound?*
  (/ĕ/) *Listen again:* hen. *What is the end sound?* (/n/)

- Continue, having children blend and then segment the other animal names.

 ## Phoneme Substitution

Using the animal names again, have children substitute initial sounds
to make new words. Substitute / p / for / h / in *hen* to make *pen*; / j / for
/ d / in *dog* to get *jog*; then substitute / b / for / g / in *goat* to get *boat*.

 Sunshine State Standards pp. T16–T17
★ = FCAT Benchmark in Gr. 3–5

★LA.A.1.1.2.K.5 basic phonetic principles
★LA.A.1.1.2.K.6 print conveys meaning
★LA.A.1.1.3.K.4 uses sources to build vocabulary
LA.A.2.1.5.K.2 pictures, signs for information
LA.C.1.1.4.K.1 listens for specific information

Getting Ready to Learn

To help plan their day, tell children that they will

- listen to a Big Book: *Splash!*

- learn the new letters *J, j,* and
  sort words that begin with *j.*

- sort animals according to
  environments in the Science
  Center.

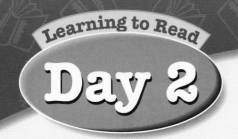
LA.C.1.1.1.K.1   LA.E.2.1.1.K.2
LA.A.1.1.1.K.1   LA.A.1.1.4.K.1
LA.C.1.1.1.K.2   ★LA.E.1.1.2.K.1

Big Book

Houghton Mifflin
Reading

Splash!

Flora McDonnell

Purposes • concepts of print • story language
• reading strategy • comprehension skill

Selection Summary
A clever and mischievous little elephant helps the animals around him cool off.

Key Concepts
Animal environments

Hot and cool

English Language Learners

LA.D.1.1.1.K.2

While reading, clarify the onomatopeic words, since these vary from language to language and may not be so obvious to English language learners. Exaggerate the sound of the word as you act it out. Have children say and act out the word with you.

Sharing the Big Book
Oral Language/Comprehension

▶ Building Background

Introduce the Big Book by reading the title and the names of the author and illustrator. Ask children how they cool off when they are hot. Then discuss how different kinds of animals might stay cool.

Strategy: Question

Teacher Modeling Do a picture walk through pages 2–7. Then model how to pose questions to make reading the story even more interesting.

> **Think Aloud**
>
> *As I read, I ask myself questions about what is happening. Then I try to find the answers. So far, I know this book is about animals. I'll ask myself: What will the problem be in the story? How will the animals solve it?*

Ask children what questions *they* have about the title.

Comprehension Focus:
Story Structure: Beginning, Middle, End

Teacher Modeling Remind children to look for the problem at the beginning of a story.

> **Think Aloud**
>
> *Every story has a beginning, a middle, and an end. There is usually a problem at the beginning and the solution to it at the end. Let's look for those things as we read.*

Sunshine State Standards pp. T18–T19   ★ = FCAT Benchmark in Gr. 3–5

★**LA.E.1.1.2.K.1** sequence of events, setting
LA.A.1.1.1.K.1 oral predictions
LA.A.1.1.4.K.1 strategies to comprehend text

LA.C.1.1.1.K.1 follows 2-step oral directions
LA.C.1.1.1.K.2 listens to oral language
LA.D.1.1.1.K.2 knows functions of language

▶ Sharing the Story

As you read the selection aloud, add drama and build anticipation by emphasizing the pauses between pages (marked by ellipses).

▶ Responding

Personal Response Encourage children to use the language of the story as they react to it.

- *What animals did you see in the story?*

- *How did all the animals feel at the beginning?*

- *What did the baby elephant do for them in the middle of the story?*

- *What was your favorite part of the story?*

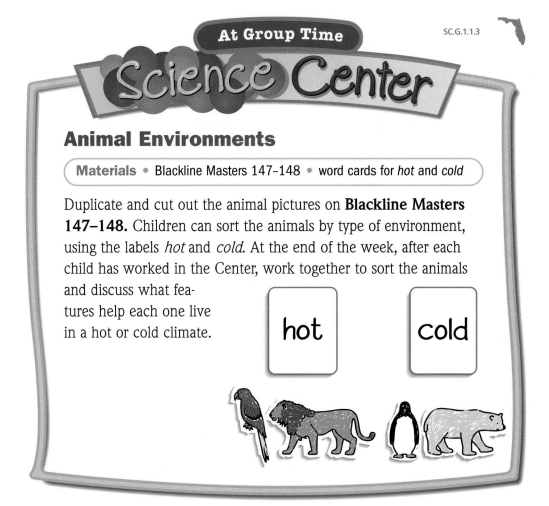

At Group Time

SC.G.1.1.3

Science Center

Animal Environments

(**Materials** • Blackline Masters 147–148 • word cards for *hot* and *cold*)

Duplicate and cut out the animal pictures on **Blackline Masters 147–148.** Children can sort the animals by type of environment, using the labels *hot* and *cold.* At the end of the week, after each child has worked in the Center, work together to sort the animals and discuss what features help each one live in a hot or cold climate.

hot   cold

Extra Support

SC.G.1.1.3

Compare this story with one about animals in a different environment. Talk with children about the types of animals and where they live.

LA.E.2.1.1.K.2 uses personal interpretations
SC.G.1.1.3 plants, animals live in environments

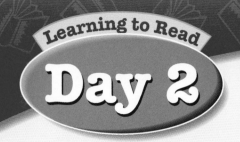
Phonics

✓ Initial Consonant j

▶ Develop Phonemic Awareness

Beginning Sound Read or sing the jingle, and have children echo it line for line. Have them listen for the /j/ words and jump for each one. See Theme Resources page R2 for music and lyrics.

Jumping Jill's Song
(Tune: "Twinkle, Twinkle, Little Star")

Jumping Jill can jump
    so high.
Jill can jump in warm July.
Jumping Jill can jump
    so low.
Jill can jump for joy,
    you know.
Join her in a jumping game.
As you jump, call out her name!

▶ Connect Sounds to Letters

Beginning Letter Display the *Jumping Jill* card, and have children name the letter on the picture. Say: *The letter j stands for the sound /j/, as in* jump. *When you see a j, remember Jumping Jill. That will help you remember the sound /j/.*

Write *jump* on the board. Underline the *j*. *What is the first letter in the word* jump? *(j)* Jump *starts with /j/, so j is the first letter I write for* jump.

Compare and Review: r, z In the pocket chart, display the Letter Cards as shown and the Picture Cards in random order. Review the sounds for *j*, *r*, and *z*. In turn, children can name a picture, say the beginning sound, and put the card below the right letter.

Tell children that they will sort more pictures in the Phonics Center today.

OBJECTIVES

Children

• identify words that begin with /j/

• identify pictures whose names start with the letter *j*

• form the letters *J, j*

MATERIALS

• **Alphafriend** *Jumping Jill*

• **Letter Cards** *j, r, z*

• **Picture Cards** for *j, r, z*

• **Blackline Master** 166

• **Phonics Center:** Theme 10, Week 1, Day 2

Extra Support

★LA.A.1.1.2.K.3

To help children remember the sound for *j*, point out that the letter's name gives a clue to its sound: *j*, /j/.

English Language Learners

★LA.A.1.1.2.K.3

If English language learners are having difficulty with the /j/ sound, provide extra practice. Display Picture Cards for *j* and have fluent speakers work with children in pairs to model. If children confuse /j/ with /s/ or /y/, say words with initial /sh/, /y/, or /j/, and have children show "thumbs up" when they hear /j/.

Sunshine State Standards pp. T20–T21   ★ = FCAT Benchmark in Gr. 3–5

★**LA.A.1.1.2.K.2** knows alphabet
★**LA.A.1.1.2.K.3** knows sounds of alphabet
★**LA.A.1.1.2.K.5** basic phonetic principles

▶ Handwriting

Writing J, j Tell children that now they'll learn to write the letters that stand for /j/: capital *J* and small *j.* Write each letter as you recite the handwriting rhyme. Chant the rhyme as children "write" the letter in the air.

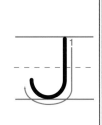

Handwriting Rhyme: J

Down from the top,
Then a short curve
Bring it up a little,
Just a little swerve:
It's a *J*, big *J*, big *J*!

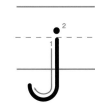

Handwriting Rhyme: j

Small *j* has
Just one line down.
Curve up a little.
Add a dot as a crown:
It's a *j*, small *j*, small *j*!

▶ Apply

Practice Book page 287 Children will complete the page at small group time.

Blackline Master 166 This page provides additional handwriting practice for small group time.

★LA.A.1.1.2.K.2, 3, 5

Phonics Center

Use the Phonics Center materials for **Theme 10, Week 1, Day 2.**

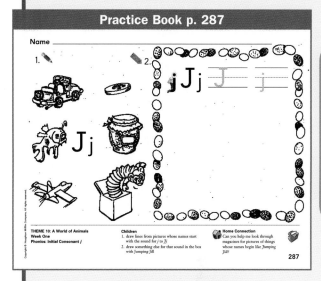

Teacher's Note

Handwriting practice for the continuous stroke style is available on **Blackline Master 192.**

Portfolio Opportunity

Save the **Practice Book** page to show children's grasp of the letter-sound association.
Save **Blackline Master 166** for a handwriting sample.

DAY 2

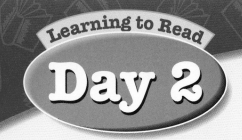

Learning to Read
Day 2

Teacher's Note

Prepare word cards for the decodable words *cat, fox,* and *hen* for this activity.

✔ High-Frequency Word
New Word: are

▶ Teach

Tell children that today they will learn to read and write a word that they will often see in stories. Say *are* and use it in context.

We *are* playing ball.   The cats *are* in the house.   *Are* you coming today?

Write *are* on the board, and have children spell it as you point to the letters. Say, **Spell** *are* **with me,** **a-r-e.** Then lead children in a chant, clapping on each beat, to help them remember the spelling: **a-r-e, are! a-r-e, are!**

Word Wall   Post *are* on the Word Wall, and remind children to look there when they need to remember how to write the word.

▶ Practice

Reading Build sentences in a pocket chart as shown. Children take turns reading. Place the pocket chart in the Phonics Center so that children can practice building and reading sentences.

Sunshine State Standards pp. T22–T23   ★ = FCAT Benchmark in Gr. 3–5

★**LA.A.1.1.3.K.1** identifies high-frequency words
★**LA.A.1.1.3.K.4** uses sources to build vocabulary

Display page 7 of *Higglety Pigglety: A Book of Rhymes.*

■ Share the poem "Crackers and Crumbs."

■ Reread the first line of the poem, tracking the print. Have children point to the word *are* when you come to it.

Higglety Pigglety: A Book of Rhymes, page 7

▶ **Apply**

Practice Book page 288 Children will read and write *are* as they complete the Practice Book page. On Day 3, they will practice reading *are* in the **Phonics Library** story "Ken and Jen."

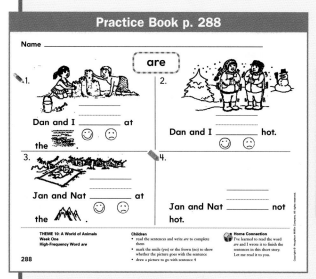

Practice Book p. 288

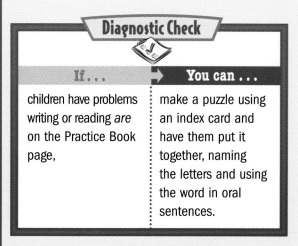

Diagnostic Check

If . . .	You can . . .
children have problems writing or reading *are* on the Practice Book page,	make a puzzle using an index card and have them put it together, naming the letters and using the word in oral sentences.

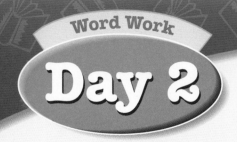

Word Work

Day 2

★LA.A.1.1.3.K.1
LA.B.2.1.2.K.1
LA.B.1.1.3.K.1

High-Frequency Word Practice

▶ Building Sentences

Make a word card for *fox*. Then tell children you want to build a sentence about animals in a zoo.

■ Display the Word and Picture Cards in random order. Put the words *A fox* in the pocket chart, and read them. Point out that as the first word in your sentence, *A*, is spelled with a capital letter.

■ *I want the next word to be* and. *Who can find that word?*

■ Continue building *A fox and a* _____ *are at the (zoo)*. Children can choose an animal picture card for the blank. Read the completed sentence together.

■ Ask children to suggest other zoo animals. Write each word on a card and add a sketch, if possible. Children can use the new cards for animal names in the sentence and take turns reading.

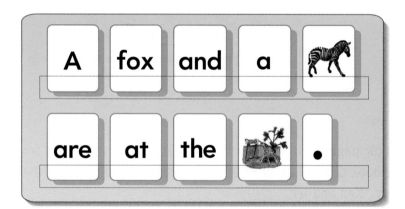

 **Writing Opportunity** Each child can use the pocket chart sentence as a model and add his or her own drawings to complete it. Some children may wish to use words instead of pictures in their sentences. Remind those children to use temporary phonics spellings by saying the words slowly and writing the letters they hear.

OBJECTIVES

Children

• read high-frequency words

• create and write sentences with high-frequency words

MATERIALS

• **Word Cards** *A, a, and, are, the*

• **Picture Cards** *hen, otter, yak, zebra, zoo*

• **Punctuation Card:** period

 **Teacher's Note**

You will need word cards for *at* and *for* to build the sample sentence.

Sunshine State Standards pp. T24–T25   ★ = FCAT Benchmark in Gr. 3–5

★**LA.A.1.1.3.K.1** identifies high-frequency words   **LA.C.1.1.4.K.1** listens for specific information
LA.B.1.1.3.K.1 uses spelling approximations   **LA.C.3.1.1.K.1** speaks clearly, loudly
LA.B.2.1.2.K.1 writes with pictures, words

Writing & Language

LA.C.1.1.4.K.1

Vocabulary Expansion

> ## Comparing Information

Tell children that they can learn new information from what they read. *In Splash!, what kinds of real animals did we read about? What did you learn about them?*

Listening Read the poem "Giraffes Don't Huff" on page 42 of *Higglety Pigglety,* and ask children to listen for new information about giraffes.

- On divided chart paper, write the stems *Giraffes do...* and *Giraffes do not....*

- Help children recall information from the poem. List their ideas in the appropriate sections of the chart.

- Continue, listing information about some other animals children read about this week.

Giraffes do...
eat green leaves
keep quiet

Giraffes do not...
huff
hoot
roar

Elephants do...
trumpet
cool off in water

Elephants do not...
roar
climb trees

At Group Time

LA.C.3.1.1.K.1

Dramatic Play Center

Materials • audiotape of loud/soft everyday sounds • Blackline Masters 149–150

If possible, prepare an audiotape of everyday sounds from home and school for children to listen to during this activity. Choose a mix of loud and soft sounds.

Divide several sheets of paper in half with a solid line. Label one side "Loud" and the other side "Not Loud." Partners can cut out pictures from **Blackline Masters 149–150,** take turns pantomiming and imitating the sound each animal or object makes, and paste the picture in the appropriate category.

Loud | Not Loud

OBJECTIVES

Children
- compare information

MATERIALS

- *Higglety Pigglety: A Book of Rhymes,* page 42

DAY 2

Day 3

Day at a Glance

Learning to Read

Big Book:

Splash!

☑ **Phonics:**
Blending *j*
-ug, *page T34*

Word Work

Building Words, *page T36*

Writing & Language

Shared Writing, *page T37*

Managing Small Groups

Teacher-Led Group
- Read **Phonics Library** selection "Ken and Jen."
- Write letters *U, u;* begin **Blackline Masters** **177 or 203.**
- Begin *Practice Book,* 289–290.

Independent Groups
- Finish **Blackline Masters 177 or 203.** *Practice Book,* 289–290.
- Dramatic Play, Science, other Centers

Opening

LA.A.2.1.5.K.2
★LA.A.1.1.2.K.6
★LA.A.1.1.3.K.4

Calendar

Sunday	Monday	Tuesday	Wednesday	Thursday	Friday	Saturday
			1	2	3	4
5	6	7	8	9	10	11
12	13	14	15	16	17	18
19	20	21	22	23	24	25
26	27	28	29	30	31	

After naming the day and date, have children describe the weather today. Talk about how some animals hibernate, or sleep through the winter, and then become active when warmer weather comes in the spring. Ask what animals might do in very hot weather.

Daily Message

Interactive Writing Use some exact naming words for animals in today's message and talk about them. Choose children to write words they know. As you reread each sentence, point out the capital at the beginning.

We will write about <u>elephants</u> today.

Choose a volunteer to point to and read the word that was added to the wall this week. *(are) What other words begin with the same letter? What other words have three letters? What are some shorter words? What are some longer words?*

Routines

✓ Daily Phonemic Awareness
Blending and Segmenting Phonemes

- Read "Giraffes Don't Huff" on page 42 of *Higglety Pigglety.* Break apart some poem words. **Listen: /h/ /ŭ/ /f/. Say those sounds with me. Blend: /h/ /ŭ/ /f/.** (*huff*).

- *Now I'll say another word from the poem. This time, you say it slowly to yourself and hold up a finger for each sound.* Say *hoot*, stretching out the sounds. Have children count and then isolate the sounds. Continue, having children segment the sounds in *keep*.

✓ Phoneme Substitution

- *Now let's change one sound to make a new word. Listen:* huff. *Take away /h/. What is left?* (/uff/) *Now add /p/ to /uff/. What's the new word?* (*puff*) Continue with *buff, cuff, muff, ruff.*

Sunshine State Standards pp. T26–T27
★ = FCAT Benchmark in Gr. 3–5

★LA.A.1.1.2.K.5 basic phonetic principles
★LA.A.1.1.2.K.6 print conveys meaning
★LA.A.1.1.3.K.4 uses sources to build vocabulary
LA.A.2.1.5.K.2 pictures, signs for information
LA.C.1.1.4.K.1 listens for specific information

THEME 10

Giraffes Don't Huff

Giraffes don't huff or hoot or howl
They never grump, they never growl
They never roar, they never riot,
They eat green leaves
And just keep quiet.

by Karla Kuskin

42

Higglety Pigglety: A Book of Rhymes, page 42

Getting Ready to Learn

To help plan their day, tell children that they will

- reread and talk about the Big Book: *Splash!*

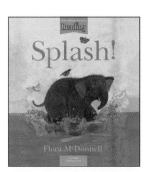

- read a story called "Ken and Jen."

Ken and Jen
by Thomas Alexander
illustrated by Thierry Courtin

- act out parts of the story in the Dramatic Play Center.

DAY 3

LA.C.1.1.1.K.2
LA.A.1.1.4.K.1

Sharing the Big Book

Big Book
Reading
Splash!

Flora McDonnell

Reading for Understanding Reread the story, emphasizing the animal naming words. Pause for discussion points.

Extra Support

★LA.A.1.1.2.K.1

Ask volunteers to show where the sentence begins on page 4. What do they notice about the first letter? Recall that a sentence always begins with a capital letter, and have children find the beginning of the next sentence on page 7.

Hot, hot, hot!
The elephants
are hot.

pages 2–3

Tiger is hot.

pages 4–5

Rhinoceros is hot.

pages 6–7

Sunshine State Standards pp. T28–T29   ★ = FCAT Benchmark in Gr. 3–5

★**LA.A.1.1.2.K.1** how print is organized
★**LA.A.2.1.1.K.1** main idea from a read aloud
★**LA.E.1.1.2.K.1** sequence of events, setting

LA.A.1.1.4.K.1 strategies to comprehend text
LA.C.1.1.1.K.2 listens to oral language

pages 8–9

pages 10–11

pages 12–13

DAY 3

▶ Supporting Comprehension

title page

Strategy: Question
LA.A.1.1.4.K.1

Teacher-Student Modeling Review the questions children asked about the title before reading yesterday.

■ *What were you curious about after reading the title and looking at the picture? ... Did you find out what was splashing? What new questions do you want answered as we reread the story today?*

pages 2–7

Comprehension Focus:
Story Structure: Beginning, Middle, End
★LA.E.1.1.2.K.1

Teacher-Student Modeling Remind children that they meet the most important characters and find out what the problem is in the beginning of a story.

■ *What animals do we meet on pages 2–7?* (Mother and Baby Elephant, Tiger, Rhinoceros) *What is their problem?* (They are all too hot.)

pages 2–3

Noting Details
★LA.A.2.1.1.K.1

■ *Look at the bodies and faces of the elephants. How can you tell they are hot or uncomfortable?* (They look tired, worn out by the heat.)

page 5

Compare and Contrast
FCAT Benchmark in Gr. 3–5

■ *How does the tiger act when it is hot? Is it the same or different from the way the elephants act? How?* (It pants and looks tired and droopy, like the elephants.)

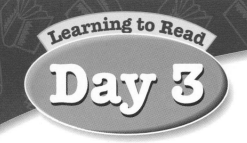

Day 3

▶ **Supporting Comprehension**

★LA.E.1.1.2.K.1

pages 14–19

Comprehension Focus:
✓ **Story Structure: Beginning, Middle, End**

Teacher-Student Modeling *What problem do the animals have at the beginning of the story? What do they do in the middle to solve their problem?* (They follow Baby Elephant to the water.) *What do they do in the water?* (They drink it, squirt it, and splash in it.)

pages 20–21
LA.C.2.1.1.K.1
Drawing Conclusions/Making Judgments

■ *Look at the expressions on the animals' faces now. How do they feel? Are they still hot? Why not?*

pages 22–23
FCAT Benchmark in Gr. 3–5
Cause/Effect

■ *Why are the animals so happy now?* (The water cooled them off.)

Oral Language
On a rereading, note interesting sound words.

Vocabulary
clever: To be clever is to show good thinking.

Splash!
goes Mother Elephant.

pages 14–15

Splosh!
goes Rhinoceros.

pages 16–17

Whoosh!
Sploosh!
goes Tiger.

pages 18–19

Sunshine State Standards pp. T30–T31   ★ = FCAT Benchmark in Gr. 3–5

★LA.A.1.1.2.K.4 concept of words, meaning   LA.C.2.1.1.K.1 main idea in nonprint
★LA.A.2.1.1.K.1 main idea from a read-aloud   LA.E.2.1.2.K.1 knows rhymes in text
★LA.E.1.1.2.K.1 sequence of events, setting

Splash!

Splash!

Splash!

Splash!

pages 20–21

Now Tiger is cool and happy.

Now Rhinoceros is cool and happy.

Now Mother Elephant is cool and happy.

pages 22–23

What a happy, cool, clever little baby elephant!

pages 24–25

▶ Supporting Comprehension

pages 22–23 ★LA.E.1.1.2.K.1

Comprehension Focus: Story Structure: Beginning, Middle, End

Student Modeling *What part of the story is this? What happens at the end?* (The animals solve their problem by cooling off in the water.) *What did Baby Elephant do at the beginning? in the middle? How did he feel at the end?*

pages 24–25 ★LA.A.2.1.1.K.1

Noting Details

■ *What is the mother elephant doing in this picture? How do you think she feels?*

pages 24–25 ★LA.A.2.1.1.K.1

Making Judgments

■ *What did Baby Elephant do that was clever?*

Revisiting the Text

page 22

Concepts of Print ★LA.A.1.1.2.K.4

✓ **Capital at the Beginning of a Sentence**

■ Have a child point to the capital letter at the beginning of the first sentence on page 22. Have another find the beginning of the next sentence. Point out the capital letter as a clue to where the sentence begins.

Challenge

LA.E.2.1.2.K.1

This book repeats many words in the same sentence. As you point to a word, some children may be able to find its match.

DAY 3

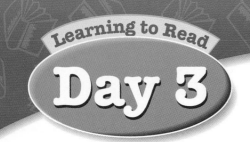

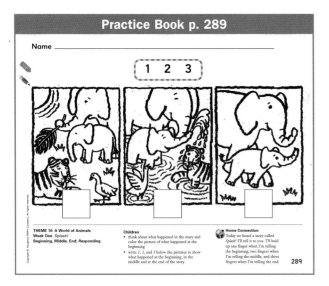

Name _____

`1  2  3`

THEME 10: A World of Animals
Week One *Splash!*
Beginning, Middle, End; Responding

Children
- think about what happened in the story and color the picture of what happened at the beginning
- write *1, 2,* and *3* below the pictures to show what happened at the beginning, in the middle and at the end of the story

Home Connection
Today we heard a story called *Splash!* I'll tell it to you. I'll hold up one finger when I'm telling the beginning, two fingers when I'm telling the middle, and three fingers when I'm telling the end.

289

▶ # Responding to the Story

LA.A.1.1.4.K.1

Retelling Use these prompts to help children retell the story:

- *Who can name the animals in the story?*

- *What was the animals' problem at the beginning?*

- *What did Baby Elephant do in the middle of the story?*

- *How was the problem solved? What were the animals doing at the end of the story?*

Practice Book page 289 Children will complete the page at small group time.

Literature Circle Have small groups discuss the kinds of animals and what they did in the water. Children can tell what they would do to cool off in the water.

Diagnostic Check

If . . .	▶ You can . . .
children need more practice in identifying events in the beginning, middle, and end of a story,	review the story in a small group. Point out the problem and the resolution for the group.

Sunshine State Standards pp. T32–T33   ★ = FCAT Benchmark in Gr. 3–5

LA.A.1.1.4.K.1 strategies to comprehend text
LA.E.2.1.1.K.2 uses personal interpretations
SC.F.1.1.5 characteristics of plants, animals

At Group Time
Dramatic Play Center

LA.E.2.1.1.K.2

Have individuals and pairs of children take turns dramatizing the beginning, the middle, and the end of the story. Observers can guess which part of the story is being dramatized. Then children can dramatize their own warm-weather activities.

At Group Time
Science Center

SC.F.1.1.5

Prepare a simple comparison chart of the story animals' features. Have children examine the animals in *Splash!* and in picture dictionaries or other sources and put check marks beside the features each animal has. Encourage children to use the chart to talk about how the animals are alike and different.

	Elephant	Tiger	Rhinoceros
fur		√	
tail	√	√	√
hoofs	√		√
paws		√	
whiskers		√	
trunk	√		
horn			√

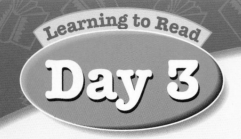
★LA.A.1.1.2.K.3, 5
★LA.A.1.1.3.K.4

Phonics

✓ *Blending* j -ug

▶ Connect Sounds to Letters

Review Consonant *j* Play Jumping Jill's song, and have children jump for each /j/ word. Write *J* and *j* on the board, and list words from the song.

Blending -ug Tell children that they'll build a word with *j*, but first they'll learn about a vowel ("helper letter"). Display Alphafriend *Umbie Umbrella.* Play Umbie Umbrella's song. (See Theme Resources page R3 for music and lyrics.)

This character is an umbrella. Say Umbie Umbrella *with me. Umbie's letter is the vowel* u, *and one sound that* u *stands for is /ŭ/.* Hold up the Letter Card *u. Say /ŭ/. Listen for /ŭ/ in these words: /ŭ/ under, /ŭ/ up, /ŭ/ us.*

Hold up Letter Card *g* and review its sound. Tell children that they know the letters and sounds they need to build *jug.* Stretch out the sounds: /j//ŭ//g/. Build *jug* letter by letter. Point to each letter and have children blend with you, sound by sound. Then have children blend the sounds as you point.

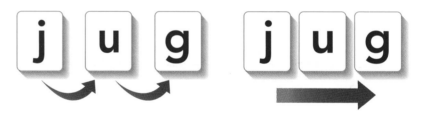

Blending -ug Words Replace *j* with *b*, and model blending /b//ug/, *bug.*

Word Wall Add *bug* to the Word Wall. Children will use *bug* to make rhyming words.

▶ Apply

Practice Book page 290 Children complete the page at small group time.

Practice Book p. 290

Name _____

j	m	r

	u	g
	u	g
	u	g

See the cat and the
_____?

The big _____ can
go here.

Here is my _____.

THEME 10: A World of Animals
Week One
Phonics: *j, -ug*

Children
• write letters to complete the picture names *(rug, jug, mug)*
• write each word to complete the sentences that go with the pictures

Home Connection
Let's think of some words that end with the sounds at the end of *rug, jug,* and *mug.* Then we can make up some silly rhymes with the words.

290

Extra Support

★LA.A.1.1.2.K.5

Read the title from "To Market, To Market," page 31 of *Higglety Pigglety: A Book of Rhymes.* Have children find a word that starts with /j/ on the page by looking for the initial *J* or *j.* Write *j* on a card, and have children find more *j*'s in books and charts around the room.

T34   THEME 10: **A World of Animals**

Sunshine State Standards pp. T34–T35   ★ = FCAT Benchmark in Gr. 3–5

★LA.A.1.1.2.K.1 how print is organized
★LA.A.1.1.2.K.3 knows sounds of alphabet
★LA.A.1.1.2.K.5 basic phonetic principles
★LA.A.1.1.3.K.1 identifies high-frequency words
★LA.A.1.1.3.K.4 uses sources to build vocabulary
LA.A.1.1.1.K.1 oral predictions

★LA.A.1.1.2.K.1, 5
LA.A.1.1.1.K.1
★LA.A.1.1.3.K.1

Phonics in Action

Phonics Library

A World of Animals

Reading

Phonics/Decoding Strategy

Teacher-Student Modeling Discuss using the Phonics/Decoding Strategy to read words in the title.

Think Aloud

The title begins with capital K. The sound for K is /k/. I know the sounds for e, n: /ĕ//n/, -en. Let's blend: /k//en/, Ken. Is Ken a real word? Does it make sense here? Who is Ken?

Have children read the rest of the title silently. Ask volunteers to read the whole title and tell how they blended the girl's name.

Do a picture walk. Show children that Ken dug a pit on page 2. Write *dug* on the board; model saying the three sounds and then blend /d//ug/, *dug.* Ask one child to point and model blending. Ask if the word would make sense in a story about children who dug a pit in the sand.

▶ Coached Reading

Have children read each page silently before reading with you. Prompts:

pages 2–3 *What are Ken and Jen doing at the beginning of the story?*

page 4 Have volunteers model how they blended *dug*. Then ask: *What two words on this page rhyme? What letters are the same in those words?*

page 5 *What is Ken and Jen's problem here in the middle of the story?*

pages 6–7 *Who solves the problem at the end of the story? How?*

Purposes
- apply phonics skills
- apply high-frequency words

Ken and Jen
by Thomas Alexander
illustrated by Thierry Courtin

1

Ken dug a big pit.
Dig, Ken, dig.

Jen dug a big pit.
Dig, Jen, dig.

2   3

Ken dug.
Jen dug.

It is hot, hot, hot!

4   5

🐕 is wet.

Ken and Jen are wet.

6   7

Home Connection

Children can color the pictures in the take-home version of "Ken and Jen." After rereading on Day 4, they can take it home to read to family members.

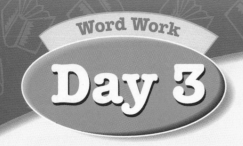

Word Work

Day 3

OBJECTIVES

Children

- blend initial consonants with -*ug* to read words

MATERIALS

- **Letter Cards** *b, d, g, h, j, r, t, u*

★LA.A.1.1.2.K.5
★LA.A.1.1.3.K.4

Building Words

▶ Word Family: -*ug*

Using the Letter Cards, model how to build *bug*. *First I'll stretch out the sounds:* /b//ŭ//g/. *How many sounds do you hear? The first sound is* /b/. *I'll put up a* b *to spell that. The next sound is* /ŭ/. *What letter spells that? The last sound is* /g/. *What letter should I choose for that?*

Next, remove the *b* and ask what sounds are left. *Which letter should I add to build* jug? Model how to read *jug* by blending /j/ with /ug/.

Continue making and blending -*ug* words by substituting *d, h, r,* and *t.*

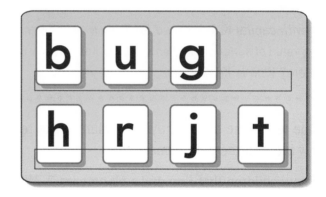

Have small groups work together to build -*ug* words. They can use block letters or other manipulative letters in your collection.

(T36) **THEME 10: A World of Animals**

Sunshine State Standards pp. T36–T37   ★ = FCAT Benchmark in Gr. 3–5

★**LA.A.1.1.2.K.5** basic phonetic principles   **LA.B.1.1.3.K.3** uses end punctuation
★**LA.A.1.1.3.K.4** uses sources to build vocabulary   **LA.B.2.1.2.K.1** writes with pictures, words
LA.B.1.1.3.K.2 directionality of print   **LA.C.2.1.1.K.1** main idea in nonprint

Shared Writing

▶ Writing a Report

Viewing and Speaking Page through the Big Book *Splash!* with children, asking what they notice about elephants.

- Tell children they can learn a lot about an animal by looking at a picture of it. Explain that they can share what they know with others by writing the information in a *report*.

- Write the title and topic sentence as shown, and discuss them with children.

- Explain that now you will write the sentences they say about elephants. Review the pictures of elephants in the book. Ask volunteers to say one sentence about elephants from looking at the picture.

- Write children's responses. As needed, prompt with questions about the animal's size, color, and special features.

- Model how to start each sentence with a capital letter and how to end it with a period. Encourage children to show you where to leave spaces between words and to name letters they know.

Elephants

We know a lot about elephants.
Elephants are big animals.
Elephants are gray.
Elephants have wrinkly skin.
Elephants have trunks.
Elephants like to squirt water.

OBJECTIVES

Children

- think of words and sentences for an informational report
- participate in shared writing

MATERIALS

- **Big Book:** *Splash!*

DAY 3

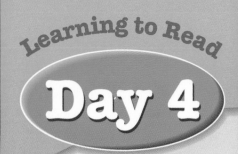

Learning to Read

Day 4

Day at a Glance

Learning to Read

Big Book:

Baby Animals Play

 Phonics:
Reviewing
/ j /; Blending
-*ug* Words,
page T42

Word Work

Building Words, *page T44*

Writing & Language

Interactive Writing, *page T45*

Managing Small Groups

Teacher-Led Group
- Reread **Phonics Library** selection "Ken and Jen."
- Begin *Practice Book,* 291.

Independent Groups
- Finish *Practice Book,* 291.
- **Phonics Center:** Theme 10, Week 1, Day 4
- Writing, other Centers

Opening

LA.A.2.1.5.K.2
★LA.A.1.1.2.K.6
★LA.A.1.1.3.K.4

Calendar

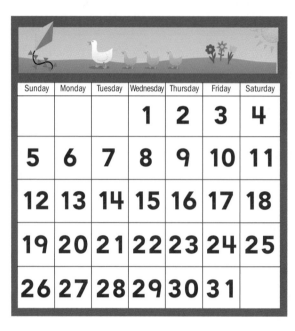

Sunday	Monday	Tuesday	Wednesday	Thursday	Friday	Saturday
			1	2	3	4
5	6	7	8	9	10	11
12	13	14	15	16	17	18
19	20	21	22	23	24	25
26	27	28	29	30	31	

Review the letters that spell the name of the month. For each letter in the word, ask children to think of another word that begins with that letter.

Daily Message

Interactive Writing Have volunteers contribute letters and words to the message. Encourage them to show where to leave spaces between words.

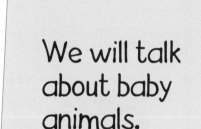

We will talk about baby animals.

Remind children that the words on the Word Wall are in ABC order. Tell them you will say the alphabet slowly, and ask them to raise their hand when you come to a letter that begins a word on the wall. **A... are there any words that begin with a? Who will point to them and read them?**

Routines

 ## Daily Phonemic Awareness
Blending and Segmenting Phonemes

Read "Bugs" on pages 46–47 of *Higglety Pigglety.* Tell children you will break apart a word from the poem. **Listen: /b//ŭ//g/.** Ask children to say the sounds and then blend them to make a word. *(bug)* Repeat.

- *Now I'll say another word. You say it slowly and hold up a finger for each sound. Listen.* Have children tell how many sounds are in *bad* and isolate the first, middle, and end sounds.

Phoneme Substitution

- *Let's change one sound to make a new word. Listen: bug. Take away /b/. What is left?* (/ug/) *Add /h/ to /ug/. What's the word?* (hug)

- Continue, substituting /b/ for /m/ in *mean* to get *bean* and /s/ for /b/ in *bad* to get *sad.*

Higglety Pigglety: A Book of Rhymes, pages 46–47

Getting Ready to Learn

To help plan their day, tell children that they will

- read the Science Link: *Baby Animals Play.*

- learn to make and read new words in the Phonics Center.

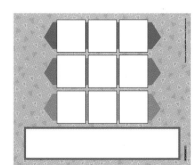

- read a book called "Ken and Jen."

Sunshine State Standards pp. T38–T39
★ = FCAT Benchmark in Gr. 3–5

★LA.A.1.1.2.K.5 basic phonetic principles
★LA.A.1.1.2.K.6 print conveys meaning
★LA.A.1.1.3.K.4 uses sources to build vocabulary
LA.A.2.1.5.K.2 pictures, signs for information
LA.C.1.1.4.K.1 listens for specific information

DAY 4

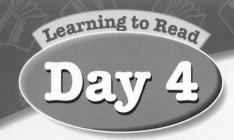
SC.F.1.1.3, 5
LA.A.1.1.1.K.1
LA.A.1.1.1.K.1

FCAT Benchmark in Gr. 3–5
LA.A.1.1.4.K.1

Sharing the Big Book
Science Link

▶ Building Background

Let children with cats or dogs describe their pets. *Has anyone had dogs (cats) since they were puppies (kittens)? What were the baby animals like? What other things do you know about baby animals?* Explain that baby animals play in different ways and that this is how they learn.

Reading for Understanding Pause for discussion as you share the selection.

---

title page
Strategy: Question

Student Modeling *What are you curious about as you look at the title page? What questions will you ask yourself about the animals? Watch for the answers as we read.*

---

title page
Main Idea

- *How does the title of this selection help us know what it's about?*

pages 32–33
Compare and Contrast

- *What do you call this baby animal on page 32?* (a colt) *What do you call the animals on page 33?* (cubs) *What do all these animals do that is the same? that is different?*

OBJECTIVES

Children

- identify the beginning, middle, and end of the story
- recognize that a capital letter begins a sentence

Big Book
Baby Animals Play

Splash!
Flora McDonnell

pages 29–35

English Language Learners

★LA.A.1.1.3.K.3

Help English language learners to create a chart of Animal Baby Names: *cat/kitten, dog/puppy, zebra/colt, tiger/cub, elephant/calf, duck/duckling, pig/piglet, goat/kid.* Have children illustrate the chart and post it in the Writing Center. Children can add to the chart as they learn more animal names.

Sunshine State Standards pp. T40–T41   ★ = FCAT Benchmark in Gr. 3–5

★LA.A.1.1.2.K.4 concept of words, meaning   LA.A.1.1.1.K.1 oral predictions
★LA.A.1.1.3.K.2 identifies noun words   LA.A.1.1.4.K.1 strategies to comprehend text
★LA.A.1.1.3.K.3 sorts words from categories   SC.F.1.1.3 describes organism growth

What is a baby cat?
A kitten!
This kitten likes to climb.

What is a baby dog?
A puppy!
This puppy likes to chew.

pages 30–31

What is a baby zebra?
A colt!
This colt likes to run.

What is a baby tiger?
A cub!
This cub likes to wrestle.

pages 32–33

What is a baby elephant?
A calf!
This calf likes to splash.

Here are more baby animals.
Do you know their names?

1. duckling
2. piglet
3. kid

pages 34–35

pages 34–35

Concepts of Print ★LA.A.1.1.2.K.4

Capital at the Beginning of a Sentence

■ Reread the first word of one of the questions, pointing to the word as you read. Ask: *What is the first letter in this word? Is it a capital or a small letter? Why?* Continue with another sentence, asking a volunteer to point to and identify the first letter and tell whether it is a capital or small letter.

page 35

Prior Knowledge LA.A.1.1.1.K.1

■ Invite children to name any of the baby animals they recognize. Read aloud the numbered answers and show children how they match the pictures.

▶ Responding LA.A.1.1.4.K.1

Summarizing Talk with children about the baby animals in the book. Have children summarize the selection, using the pictures as prompts. Reread the last page, allowing time for responses to the question. Ask children what animal they enjoyed reading about the most.

DAY 4

 Challenge

★LA.A.1.1.3.K.2

For children who are ready for a challenge, make word cards for all the baby animal names. Have children find the words in the book by matching the cards to the words in print.

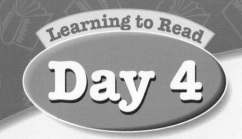

Learning to Read
Day 4

Phonics

Blending -ug Words

▶ **Connect Sounds to Letters**

Review Consonant j Using self-stick notes, cover the words on page 11 of *From Apples to Zebras: A Book of ABC's.* Then display the page. Ask children to identify each picture and tell what letter they expect to see first in each word and why. Uncover the words so that children can check their predictions.

From Apples to Zebras: A Book of ABC's, page 11

Reviewing -ug Remind children that to build some words with *j*, they also need a vowel ("helper letter"), because every word has at least one of those. Ask which Alphafriend stands for the vowel sound /ŭ/. (Umbie Umbrella) Display Umbie and have children think of other words that start with /ŭ/. (*under, up, us,* and *uncle*)

Hold up Letter Cards *b, u,* and *g. Watch and listen as I build a word from the Word Wall: /b//ŭ//g/, bug, /b//ŭ//g/, bug.*

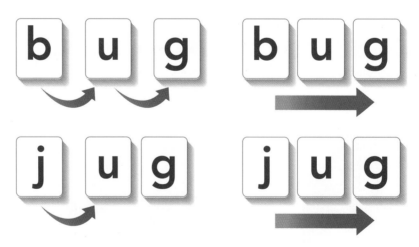

Blending -ug Words Place the Letter Card *j* in front of *-ug. Now let's blend my new word: /j//ug/, jug.* Continue, having volunteers build and blend *hug* and *rug*.

OBJECTIVES

Children

- identify initial *j* for words that begin with /j/
- blend *j* and other initial consonants with *-ug*

MATERIALS

- ***From Apples to Zebras: A Book of ABC's,*** page 11
- **Alphafriend Card** *Umbie Umbrella*
- **Letter Cards** *b, g, h, r, u*
- **Word Cards** *A, a, I*
- **Punctuation Cards:** period
- **Phonics Center:** Theme 10, Week 1, Day 4

Teacher's Note

You will need a word card for *can* to build the sample sentence. During writing, children may ask how to spell words from the *-ug* family. Help children find the word *bug* on the Word Wall and replace *b* with appropriate initial consonant(s).

Sunshine State Standards pp. T42–T43   ★ = FCAT Benchmark in Gr. 3–5

★**LA.A.1.1.2.K.2** knows alphabet
★**LA.A.1.1.2.K.3** knows sounds of alphabet
★**LA.A.1.1.2.K.5** basic phonetic principles

▶ Apply

Begin a sentence with the first two Word Cards shown. Help children read the words. Continue building the sentence; for *hug* and *bug,* ask what letter you need to spell each sound.

Now have children rearrange the cards to make this sentence: A *bug* can *hug.* Remind them to spell the first word with a capital letter. Have volunteers read the sentence and blend the *-ug* words.

Practice Book page 291 Children will complete this page at small group time.

Phonics Library In groups today, children will also read *-ug* words as they reread the **Phonics Library** story "Ken and Jen." See suggestions, page T35.

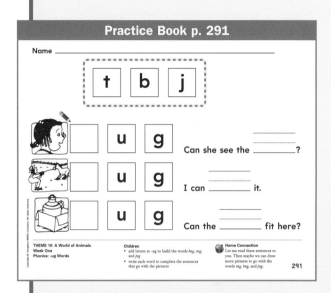

Practice Book p. 291

At Group Time

★LA.A.1.1.2.K.2, 3, 5

Phonics Center

Use Phonics Center materials for **Theme 10, Week 1, Day 4.**

DAY 4

Diagnostic Check

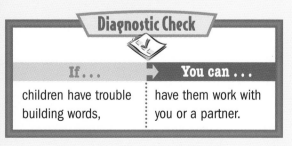

If . . .	You can . . .
children have trouble building words,	have them work with you or a partner.

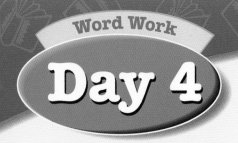

Word Work

Day 4

OBJECTIVES

Children

- build and read -ug, -et, -en words

MATERIALS

- **Letter Cards** b, d, e, g, h, j, l, m, p, r, t, u, v

Building Words

▶ Word Families: -ug, -et, -en

■ Model how to build *bug* in the pocket chart. ***First I'll stretch out the sounds: / b /... / ŭ /... / g /. How many sounds do you hear? The first sound is / b /. What letter should I choose for that?*** Continue with letters for the remaining sounds. Then replace the *b* with known consonants (*h, j, r*), building other *-ug* words for children to identify.

■ Next, use Letter Cards to build *wet*, stretching out the sounds and having children tell you what letters to use. Continue building new words by substituting the initial consonants *m, j, p, v*.

■ Repeat, this time building *ten* and making new words by substituting initial consonants *d, h, m,* and *p*.

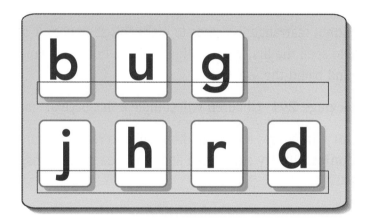

Have groups of children write *-ug, -et,* and *-en* words on index cards. They can keep a box of words they have learned to build and read.

Sunshine State Standards pp. T44–T45   ★ = FCAT Benchmark in Gr. 3–5

★**LA.A.1.1.2.K.5** basic phonetic principles   **LA.B.1.1.3.K.3** uses end punctuation
★**LA.A.1.1.3.K.1** identifies high frequency words   **LA.B.2.1.1.K.1** uses pictures, words
★**LA.A.1.1.3.K.4** uses sources to build vocabulary   **LA.B.2.1.1.K.2** ideas to shared writing

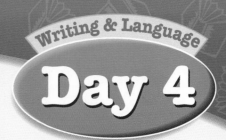

Interactive Writing

▶ Writing a Report

Remind children that you recorded information about elephants on a chart yesterday. Display the report from yesterday's shared writing. (See page T37.) Review the information, invite children to offer new information about elephants, and add sentences to the report.

Listening, Speaking, and Viewing Reread page 34 of *Baby Animals Play*, and ask if this page gives information to add. Then display more pictures of elephants and discuss them. Children can draw information from the pictures and suggest new sentences for the report.

As you write:

■ Occasionally ask volunteers to write known words.

■ Let children write the capital letter at the beginning of each new sentence and the punctuation at the end.

OBJECTIVES

Children

● record information and observations

● write letters or words in an interactive writing activity

MATERIALS

● **Big Book:** *Baby Animals Play*

Portfolio Opportunity

After displaying the finished product from a group writing activity, you might want to save it for conference time. Write contributors' names in small print next to sentences they offered for the work.

At Group Time

Writing Center

LA.B.2.1.2.K.1

Put the report in the Writing Center. Invite children to make it more interesting by creating illustrations to post next to it. Some children may want to dictate or write captions for their drawings.

Mama and her calf

DAY 4

Learning to Read
Day 5

Day at a Glance

Learning to Read

Revisiting the Literature:

Run Away! Splash!, Baby Animals Play, "Ken and Jen"

✔ **Phonics:** Review Consonants *b, c, d, f, g, h, j, k, l, m, n, p, q, r, s, t, v, w, x, z; Blending -ug Words;* page T50

Word Work

Building Words, *page T52*

Writing & Language

Independent Writing, *page T53*

Managing Small Groups

Teacher-Led Group
- Reread familiar **Phonics Library** selections.
- Begin *Practice Book, 292,* **Blackline Master 36.**

Independent Groups
- Reread **Phonics Library** selections.
- Finish *Practice Book, 292,* **Blackline Master 36.**
- Centers

Opening

LA.A.2.1.5.K.2
★LA.A.1.1.2.K.6
★LA.A.1.1.3.K.4

Calendar

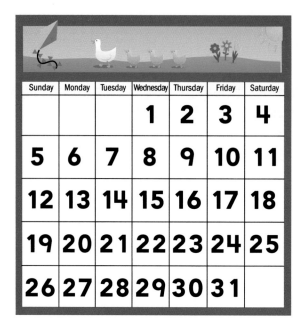

Sunday	Monday	Tuesday	Wednesday	Thursday	Friday	Saturday
			1	2	3	4
5	6	7	8	9	10	11
12	13	14	15	16	17	18
19	20	21	22	23	24	25
26	27	28	29	30	31	

Review the week's activities. Have volunteers recall the books or the animals they read about each day of the week.

Daily Message

Modeled Writing As you begin writing each word of the daily message, ask whether to write a capital or a small letter. Stress the use of small letters except the ones at the beginning of a sentence or a name.

Marita likes the elephants we read about yesterday. Daniel and Brendan like the baby animals.

Read the Word Wall together. Then play a rhyming game: *I'm going to find a word on the wall that rhymes with* hug. Bug *rhymes with* hug. *Now raise your hand when you find a word that rhymes with* car.

Daily Phonemic Awareness
Blending and Segmenting Phonemes

Display the Picture Cards *dog, goat,* and *yak.* Then play a blending game.

- *I'll say some sounds. You put them together to name one of the animals: / g /...*
  / ō /.../ t /. (goat) *Now it's your turn. Say goat slowly, stretching out the sounds.*
  Have children isolate the beginning, middle, and end sounds. Continue, having
  children blend and then segment *dog* and *yak.*

 ## Phoneme Substitution

Have children substitute initial sounds to make new words.

- *If we take away the, / g / in goat, what is left?* (-oat) *Now add / b / to*
  / oat /. What new word do we get? Say: / g // oat /, goat; / b // oat /, boat.

- Continue, having children substitute / l / for / d / in *dog* to get *log;*
  then substitute / p / for / y / in *yak* to get *pack.*

Sunshine State Standards pp. T46–T47
★ = FCAT Benchmark in Gr. 3–5

★**LA.A.1.1.2.K.5** basic phonetic principles
★**LA.A.1.1.2.K.6** print conveys meaning
★**LA.A.1.1.3.K.4** uses sources to build vocabulary
LA.A.2.1.5.K.2 pictures, signs for information
LA.C.1.1.4.K.1 listens for specific information

Getting Ready to Learn

To help plan their day, tell children that they will

- reread and talk about the books they've read this week.

- take home a story they can read.

- write a report in their journals.

Ken and Jen
by Thomas Alexander
illustrated by Thierry Courtin

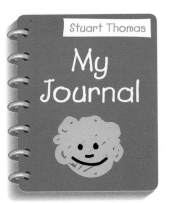

DAY 5

★LA.A.2.1.1.K.1   LA.A.1.1.4.K.1
LA.C.3.1.2.K.1   ★LA.E.1.1.2.K.1
★LA.A.1.1.2.K.5

Revisiting the Literature

▶ **Literature Discussion**

Today children will compare the books you shared this week: *Run Away!*, *Splash!*, *Baby Animals Play,* and "Ken and Jen." First, use these suggestions to help children recall the selections:

■ Have volunteers tell why the animals were unhappy at the beginning of *Splash!* and what clever animal helped them.

■ Page through the Link *Baby Animals Play.* Then have volunteers tell what some of the baby animals are called and what they like to play.

■ Read the last page of *Run Away!* and ask why the animals might have felt foolish.

■ Ask what the children did in "Ken and Jen." Write *dug* on the board and ask volunteers how they blended the sounds.

■ Ask children which book showed their favorite animal(s). After they vote on their favorite book of the week, read the text of the winner aloud.

✓ Comprehension Focus:
Story Structure: Beginning, Middle, End

Comparing Books Remind children that they have learned that most stories have a beginning, a middle, and an end. Browse through *Run Away!* with children and talk about each part: What happened in the beginning? in the middle? at the end? Remind children that the problem of the story is usually found at the beginning and the solution is often at the end.

Technology

LA.B.2.1.3.K.1

www.eduplace.com
Log on to Education Place for more activities relating to *A World of Animals.*

www.bookadventure.org
This Internet reading-incentive program provides thousands of titles for children to read.

Sunshine State Standards pp. T48–T49   ★ = FCAT Benchmark in Gr. 3–5

★LA.A.1.1.2.K.5 basic phonetic principles   LA.A.1.1.4.K.1 strategies to comprehend text
★LA.A.2.1.1.K.1 main idea from a read-aloud   LA.A.2.1.2.K.1 reads for pleasure
★LA.E.1.1.2.K.1 sequence of events, setting   LA.B.2.1.3.K.1 uses computer for writing

Building Fluency

▶ Rereading Familiar Texts

Phonics Library: "Ken and Jen" Remind children that they've learned the new word *are* this week and that they've learned to read words with *-ug*. As they reread the **Phonics Library** story "Ken and Jen," have children look for words with *-ug*.

Review Feature several **Phonics Library** titles in the Book Corner. Have children demonstrate their growing skills by choosing one to reread aloud, alternating pages with a partner. From time to time, choose specific children to point out words or phrases.

Oral Reading Learning to decode words automatically helps children read with more fluency. During phonics lessons and word building activities, tell children that this practice with the letter sounds will help them when they read stories on their own.

Ken and Jen
by Thomas Alexander
illustrated by Thierry Courtin

Ben
by Ann Spivey
illustrated by Susan Calitri

Pig Can Get Wet
by Ann Spivey
illustrated by Vincent Andriani

Blackline Master 36 Children complete the page and take it home to share their reading progress.

My Reading Log

I can read

My new words

are bug

Leveled Books

The materials listed below provide reading practice for children at different levels.

Little Big Books

Splash!
Flora McDonnell

Little Readers for Guided Reading

Houghton Mifflin Classroom Bookshelf

Home Connection

Remind children to share the take-home version of "Ken and Jen" with their families.

Revisiting the Literature/ Building Fluency

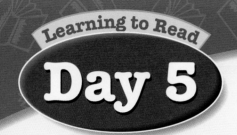

Phonics Review

✓ Consonants, Word Families

▶ Review

Tell children that they will take turns being word builders and word readers today. Have a group of word builders stand with you at the chalkboard. Others write at their work stations.

- ■ *Let's build* bug. *First, count the sounds …. I know* b *stands for /b/,* u *stands for /ŭ/, and* g *stands for /g/.* Write the letters.

- ■ Children copy *bug* on the board and blend the sounds.

- ■ *Now erase the* b *and write* r *in its place.* Children check their word against yours and ask the rest of the class (word readers) what new word they've written.

- ■ A new group changes places with the first one. At your direction, they erase the *r*, write *j*, and ask the word readers to say the new word.

Repeat the process, this time building *-et* words and then *-en* words until everyone has a turn. Examples: *dug, tug, hug; wet, set, met, pet, let, get, vet; den, hen, pen, men, ten.*

Children

- build and read words with initial consonants and short *u* + *g*, short *e* + *t*, and short *e* + *n*

- make sentences with high-frequency words

MATERIALS

- **Word Cards** *a, and, are, for, go, have, here, I, is, like, my, play, said, see, She, to*

- **Picture Cards** *assorted*

- **Punctuation Card:** period

Sunshine State Standards pp. T50–T51   ★ = FCAT Benchmark in Gr. 3–5

★LA.A.1.1.2.K.3 knows sounds of alphabet   ★LA.A.1.1.3.K.1 identifies high frequency words
★LA.A.1.1.2.K.5 basic phonetic principles   LA.E.2.1.2.K.1 knows rhymes in text

High-Frequency Word Review

☑ *I, see, my, like, a, to, and, go, is, here, for, have, said, are, the, She, play*

▶ Review

Give each small group the Word Cards, Picture Cards, and Punctuation Card needed to make a sentence. Each child holds one card. Children stand and arrange themselves to make a sentence for others to read.

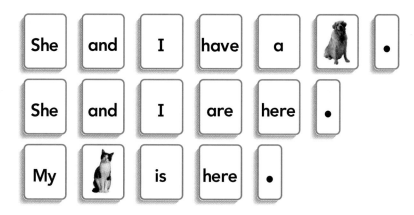

▶ Apply

Practice Book page 292 Children can complete this page independently and read it to you during small group time.

Phonics Library Have children take turns reading aloud to the class. Each child might read one page of "Ken and Jen" or a favorite **Phonics Library** selection from the previous theme. Remind readers to share the pictures!

Discussion questions:

■ *Do you hear any rhyming words in either story? What letters are the same in those words?*

■ *Find a word that starts with the same sound as Jumping Jill's name. What is the letter? What is the sound?*

■ *This week we added the word* are *to the Word Wall. Find the word* are *in "Ken and Jen."*

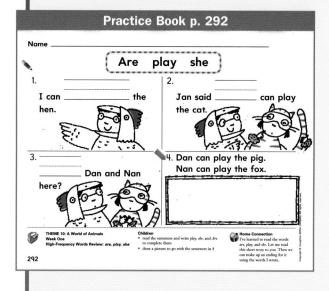

Practice Book p. 292

Portfolio Opportunity

Save the Practice Book page to show children's recognition of high-frequency words.

Diagnostic Check

If...	You can ...
children associate /j/ with *g* and not *j*,	have children say the words and point to the initial letters on the *Jj* page in *From Apples to Zebras.*
children pause at high-frequency words in **Phonics Library** selections,	have children practice finding these words with a partner on the Word Wall.

DAY 5

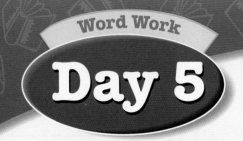

Day 5

★LA.A.1.1.2.K.5
★LA.A.1.1.3.K.4

OBJECTIVES

Children

● build and read *-et*, *-en*, and *-ug* words

MATERIALS

● **Letter Cards** *b, e, g, h, j, l, m, p, s, t, u, v, w*

Building Words

▶ ## Word Families: *-et, -en, -ug*

Along the bottom of the pocket chart, line up the letters *w, l, j, e, s,* and *g.*

Let's build the word let. *Who can tell me which letter I should use for the first sound in* let?... *the middle sound?... the last sound?*

Now ask which letter you should change to turn *let* into *jet.* Have a volunteer replace *l* with *j.* Continue building *-et* words, replacing the initial consonant with *w, g,* and *s.* On chart paper, keep a list of all the *-et* words you make, and reread the list together.

Continue the activity with *-en* words and *-ug* words. Examples: *hen, ten, men, pen; bug, hug, jug, mug, tug.*

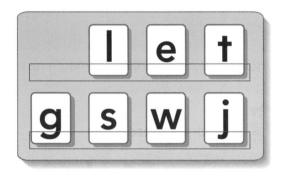

Have small groups work together to build *-ug* words on chalkboards or with manipulative letters. This time, they can add new words to the Word Bank section of their journals and add appropriate pictures.

Sunshine State Standards pp. T52–T53   ★ = FCAT Benchmark in Gr. 3–5

★**LA.A.1.1.2.K.5** basic phonetic principles
★**LA.A.1.1.3.K.4** uses sources to build vocabulary
LA.B.2.1.1.K.1 uses pictures, words

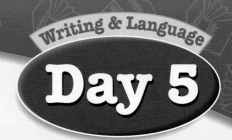
LA.B.2.1.1.K.1

Independent Writing

Journals Together, reread the charts and the report from this week's shared and interactive writing. Point out the "general word" *animals* and some of the "exact words" that name particular animals.

■ Pass out the journals.

■ *What information have we learned about animals this week? We read about some animals that live in the woods. What could you report about them in your journals? What have you learned about elephants?*

■ Suggest that children add pictures to their reports. They might draw speech balloons with sound words to show what noises their animals make.

■ Have children share what they've written. They can hold a "microphone" and pose as scientists reporting on observations they've made. Invite classmates to ask questions about the animals.

OBJECTIVES

Children
● write independently

MATERIALS

● journals
● classmade microphone

Teacher's Note

Some children will feel more comfortable sharing journal entries after they have practiced with a partner.

Literature for Week 2
Different texts for different purposes

The Tale of the Three Little Pigs

Teacher Read Aloud

Purposes

- oral language
- listening strategy
- comprehension skill

Big Books:

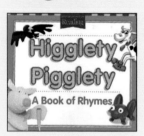

Higglety Pigglety: A Book of Rhymes

Purposes

- oral language development
- phonemic awareness

From Apples to Zebras: A Book of ABC's

Purposes

- alphabet recognition
- letters and sounds

Big Book: Main Selection

Purposes

- concepts of print
- reading strategy
- story language
- comprehension skills

Awards

- Horn Book Fanfare
- Notable Children's Trade Book in the Language Arts
- Outstanding Science Trade Book for Children
- IRA/CBC Teacher's Choice
- Library of Congress Children's Books of the Year

Also available in Little Big Book and audiotape

Leveled Books

Science Link

Which Pet?

33

Also in the Big Book:
- Science Link

Purposes
- reading strategies
- comprehension skills
- concepts of print

On My Way Practice Reader

Animals at Play
by Wil Perry
page T155

Little Readers for Guided Reading
Collection K

Houghton Mifflin Classroom Bookshelf
Level K

Phonics Library

Phonics Library

A World of Animals

Also available in Take-Home version

Purposes
- applying phonics skills and high-frequency words

Technology

www.eduplace.com
Log on to *Education Place* for more activities relating to *A World of Animals.*

www.bookadventure.org
This free Internet reading-incentive program provides thousands of titles for students to read.

Suggested Daily Routines

Instructional Goals

	Day 1	Day 2

Learning to Read

✓ *Phonemic Awareness:* Blending and Segmenting Phonemes, Phoneme Substitution

Strategy Focus: Predict/Infer

✓ *Comprehension Skill:* Compare and Contrast

✓ *Phonics Skills*

Phonemic Awareness: Beginning Sounds / l /, / b /, / k /

Initial Consonant *L, l, B, b, C, c*

Compare and Review: Initial Consonants: *b, c, l*

✓ *High-Frequency Word: he*

✓ *Concepts of Print:* End of Sentence/End Punctuation

Day 1

Opening Routines, *T60–T61*　　LA.A.2.1.5.K.2
Word Wall　　★LA.A.1.1.2.K.5, 6
　　　　　　　★LA.A.1.1.3.K.4

• **Phonemic Awareness:** Blending and Segmenting Phonemes, Phoneme Substitution　★LA.A.1.1.2.K.2, 3, 5

Teacher Read Aloud　　LA.C.1.1.1.K.1
The Tale of the Three Little Pigs, T62–T65
• **Strategy:** Predict/Infer　LA.A.1.1.1.K.1
• **Comprehension:** Compare and Contrast
　　　　　　FCAT Benchmark in Gr. 3–5

Phonics
Instruction
• Phonemic Awareness, Beginning Sound / b /, / k /, / l /, T66–T67;　★LA.A.1.1.2.K.2, 3, 5
Practice Book, 295–296

Day 2

Opening Routines, *T70–T71*　　LA.A.2.1.5.K.2
Word Wall　　★LA.A.1.1.2.K.5, 6
　　　　　　　★LA.A.1.1.3.K.4

• **Phonemic Awareness:** Blending and Segmenting Phonemes, Phoneme Substitution

Sharing the Big Book
Feathers for Lunch, T72–T73　LA.C.1.1.1.K.2
• **Strategy:** Predict/Infer　LA.A.1.1.1.K.1
• **Comprehension:** Compare and Contrast
　　　　　　FCAT Benchmark in Gr. 3–5

Phonics
Instruction, Practice
• Reviewing Initial Consonants *b, c, l, T74–T75*
　　　　　　★LA.A.1.1.2.K.2, 3, 5
• *Practice Book, 297*

High-Frequency Word
• New Word: *he, T76–T77*　★LA.A.1.1.3.K.1
• *Practice Book, 298*

Word Work

High-Frequency Word Practice: Word Families: *-ut, -ug, -et*

Day 1

High-Frequency Word Practice
• Words: *a, an, and, for, go, I, it, my, said, see, She, the, to, T68*　★LA.A.1.1.3.K.1

Day 2

High-Frequency Word Practice
• Words: *a, and, have, He, I, is, my, T78*
　　　　　　★LA.A.1.1.3.K.1

Writing & Language

Vocabulary Skill: Using Rhyming Words; Using Exact Words

Writing Skills: Writing a Book Report

Day 1

Oral Language
• Using Rhyming Words, *T69*　LA.D.2.1.2.K.1
　　　　　　　　　　　　LA.D.1.1.1.K.1

Day 2

Vocabulary Expansion　★LA.A.1.1.2.K.5
　　　　　　　　　　　★LA.A.1.1.3.K.2, 4
• Using Exact Words, Rhyming Words, *T79*
• Listening and Viewing, *T79*　LA.C.2.1.1.K.1
　　　　　　　　　　　　LA.C.1.1.4.K.1

Sunshine State Standards Achieved Each Day

LA.A = Reading
LA.B = Writing
LA.C = Listening/Viewing/Speaking
LA.D = Language
LA.E = Literature

★ = FCAT Benchmark in Grades 3–5

Day 1
★ LA.A.1.1.2.K.2 knows alphabet
★ LA.A.1.1.2.K.3 knows sounds of alphabet
★ LA.A.1.1.2.K.5 basic phonetic principles
★ LA.A.1.1.2.K.6 print conveys meaning
★ LA.A.1.1.3.K.1 identifies high frequency words
★ LA.A.1.1.3.K.4 uses sources to build vocabulary
　 LA.A.1.1.1.K.1 oral predictions
　 LA.A.2.1.5.K.2 pictures, signs for information
　 LA.C.1.1.1.K.1 follows 2-step oral directions
　 LA.D.1.1.1.K.1 knows patterns of sound
　 LA.D.2.1.2.K.1 uses repetition, rhyme in texts

Day 2
★ LA.A.1.1.2.K.2 knows alphabet
★ LA.A.1.1.2.K.3 knows sounds of alphabet
★ LA.A.1.1.2.K.5 basic phonetic principles
★ LA.A.1.1.2.K.6 print conveys meaning
★ LA.A.1.1.3.K.1 identifies high frequency words
★ LA.A.1.1.3.K.2 identifies noun words
★ LA.A.1.1.3.K.4 uses sources to build vocabulary
　 LA.A.1.1.1.K.1 oral predictions
　 LA.A.2.1.5.K.2 pictures, signs for information
　 LA.C.1.1.1.K.2 listens to oral language
　 LA.C.1.1.4.K.1 listens for specific information
　 LA.C.2.1.1.K.1 main idea in nonprint

Leveled Books, p. T105　　LA.A.2.1.2.K.1

Half-Day Kindergarten
Focus on lessons for tested skills. ✓
Then choose other activities as time allows.

Technology

Florida Lesson Planner CD-ROM
Customize your planning for *the week*
with the Florida Lesson Planner.

Key correlations are provided in
this chart. Additional correlations
are provided at point of use.

Day 3

Opening Routines, *T80–T81*   LA.A.2.1.5.K.2
                          ★ LA.A.1.1.2.K.5, 6
Word Wall   ★ LA.A.1.1.3.K.4

- **Phonemic Awareness:** Blending and
  Segmenting Phonemes, Phoneme
  Substitution   ★ LA.A.1.1.2.K.2, 3, 5

Sharing the Big Book
Feathers for Lunch, T82–T87   LA.C.1.1.1.K.2
                                LA.E.2.1.2.K.1
- **Strategy:** Predict/Infer   LA.A.1.1.1.K.1
- **Comprehension:** Compare and Contrast, *T83,
  T84, T85; Practice Book,* 299
                FCAT Benchmark in Gr. 3–5
- **Concepts of Print:** End of Sentence/End
  Punctuation, *T87*   ★ LA.A.1.1.2.K.4

Phonics

Practice, Application
- Review Consonant *c, T90–T91* ★ LA.A.1.1.2.K.2, 3, 5

Instruction   ★ LA.A.1.1.2.K.5
- Blending *-ut, T90–T91; Practice Book,* 300
- **Phonics Library:** "It Can Fit," *T91*
                          ★ LA.A.1.1.3.K.1
                          ★ LA.A.1.1.2.K.2

Building Words
- Word Family: *-ut, T92*   ★ LA.A.1.1.2.K.5
                             ★ LA.A.1.1.3.K.4

✏ **Shared Writing**   LA.E.2.1.1.K.2
- Writing a Book Report, *T93*   LA.B.2.1.2.K.1
- Viewing and Speaking, *T93*   LA.C.2.1.1.K.1

Day 4

Opening Routines, *T94–T95*   LA.A.2.1.5.K.2
                          ★ LA.A.1.1.2.K.5, 6
Word Wall   ★ LA.A.1.1.3.K.4

- **Phonemic Awareness:** Blending and
  Segmenting Phonemes, Phoneme
  Substitution   ★ LA.A.1.1.2.K.2, 3, 5

Sharing the Big Book
Science Link: "Which Pet?," *T96–T97*
                           ★ LA.A.2.1.1.K.1
- **Strategy:** Predict/Infer   LA.A.1.1.1.K.1
                        FCAT Benchmark in Gr. 3–5
- **Comprehension:** Compare and Contrast
- **Concepts of Print:** End of Sentence/End
  Punctuation   ★ LA.A.1.1.2.K.4

Phonics

Practice
- Blending *-ut* Words, *Practice Book,* 301

Building Words
- Word Families: *-ut, -ug, -et, T100*
                             ★ LA.A.1.1.2.K.5
                             ★ LA.A.1.1.3.K.4

✏ **Interactive Writing**
- Writing a Book Report, *T101*   LA.B.2.1.2.K.1
- Listening, Viewing, and Speaking, *T101*
                             LA.C.1.1.4.K.1
                             LA.C.2.1.1.K.1
                             LA.C.3.1.3.K.1

Day 5

Opening Routines, *T102–T103*   LA.A.2.1.5.K.2
                          ★ LA.A.1.1.2.K.5, 6
Word Wall   ★ LA.A.1.1.3.K.4

- **Phonemic Awareness:** Blending and
  Segmenting Phonemes, Phoneme
  Substitution

Revisiting the Literature
Comprehension: Compare and Contrast, *T104*
                          FCAT Benchmark in Gr. 3–5
Building Fluency
- **Phonics Library:** "It Can Fit," *T105*
                            LA.A.1.1.4.K.1
                          ★ LA.A.1.1.2.K.3, 5

Phonics

Review
- Consonants, Word Families, *T106* ★ LA.A.1.1.2.K.5
                             ★ LA.A.1.1.3.K.4

High-Frequency Word Review
- Words, *I, see, my, like, a, to, and, go, is, here,
  for, have, said, are, he, play, she, the, T107;*
  Practice Book, *302*   ★ LA.A.1.1.3.K.1

Building Words
- Word Families: *-ut, -ug, -et, T108*   ★ LA.A.1.1.2.K.5
                             ★ LA.A.1.1.3.K.4

✏ **Interactive Writing**
- Journals: Bird Names and Rhyming
  Words, *T109*   LA.B.2.1.2.K.1
                      LA.E.2.1.1.K.2

★ **LA.A.1.1.2.K.2** knows alphabet
★ **LA.A.1.1.2.K.3** knows sounds of alphabet
★ **LA.A.1.1.2.K.4** concept of words, meaning
★ **LA.A.1.1.2.K.5** basic phonetic principles
★ **LA.A.1.1.2.K.6** print conveys meaning
★ **LA.A.1.1.3.K.1** identifies high frequency words
★ **LA.A.1.1.3.K.4** uses sources to build vocabulary
LA.A.1.1.1.K.1 oral predictions
LA.A.2.1.5.K.2 pictures, signs for information
LA.B.2.1.2.K.1 writes with pictures, words
LA.C.1.1.1.K.2 listens to oral language
LA.C.2.1.1.K.1 main idea in nonprint
LA.E.2.1.1.K.2 uses personal interpretations
LA.E.2.1.2.K.1 knows rhymes in text

★ **LA.A.1.1.2.K.2** knows alphabet
★ **LA.A.1.1.2.K.3** knows sounds of alphabet
★ **LA.A.1.1.2.K.4** concept of words, meaning
★ **LA.A.1.1.2.K.5** basic phonetic principles
★ **LA.A.1.1.2.K.6** print conveys meaning
★ **LA.A.1.1.3.K.4** uses sources to build vocabulary
★ **LA.A.2.1.1.K.1** main idea from a read-aloud
LA.A.1.1.1.K.1 oral predictions
LA.A.2.1.5.K.2 pictures, signs for information
LA.B.2.1.2.K.1 writes with pictures, words
LA.C.1.1.4.K.1 listens for specific information
LA.C.2.1.1.K.1 main idea in nonprint
LA.C.3.1.3.K.1 uses speaking vocabulary

★ **LA.A.1.1.2.K.3** knows sounds of alphabet
★ **LA.A.1.1.2.K.5** basic phonetic principles
★ **LA.A.1.1.2.K.6** print conveys meaning
★ **LA.A.1.1.3.K.1** identifies high frequency words
★ **LA.A.1.1.3.K.4** uses sources to build vocabulary
LA.A.1.1.4.K.1 strategies to comprehend text
LA.A.2.1.5.K.2 pictures, signs for information
LA.B.2.1.2.K.1 writes with pictures, words
LA.E.2.1.1.K.2 uses personal interpretations

✏ **Independent Writing Activity, p. T109**
                               LA.B.2.1.2.K.1
                               LA.E.2.1.1.K.2

Suggested Daily Routines   (T57)

Setting up the Centers

Teacher's Note

Phonics Practice To help children celebrate the many letters and sounds they have learned this year, set up a Word Builders work space as an extension of the Phonics Center. Stock the space with magnetic letters and a cookie sheet, and index cards with initial consonants and familiar word parts. Children can "build" long lists of words they can read now.

Goldilocks and the Three Bears *by Jan Brett*
The Three Billy Goats Gruff *by Janet Stevens*
The Three Little Pigs *by James Marshall*
Three Little Kittens *by Paul Galdone*

Mouse in a house.

*LA.A.1.1.2.K.2, 3, 5

Phonics Center

Materials • Phonics Center materials for Theme 10, Week 2

Children make words with the letters *c, j, n,* and the word family -*ut* this week. They also build sentences. See pages T67, T75, and T99 for this week's activities.

LA.A.2.1.2.K.1

Book Center

Materials • books with stories of three

Put copies of stories of three in the Book Center after you've read them aloud. See the Teacher's Note on page T63 for this week's Book Center suggestion.

LA.B.2.1.2.K.1

Writing Center

Materials • crayons, markers, lined and unlined writing paper

To begin the theme, children illustrate scenes of two things whose names rhyme, add captions, and collect the pages for a class book of silly rhymes. Later children illustrate and label the important events in an animal story to make book reports. See pages T69 and T101 for the weeks Writing Center activities.

Sunshine State Standards pp. T58–T59   ★ = FCAT Benchmark in Gr. 3–5

(T58)   **THEME 10: A World of Animals**

★LA.A.1.1.2.K.2 knows alphabet   ★LA.A.1.1.2.K.5 basic phonetic principles
★LA.A.1.1.2.K.3 knows sounds of alphabet   LA.A.2.1.2.K.1 reads for pleasure

Dramatic Play Center

LA.E.2.1.1.K.2
TH.A.1.1.1

Materials • Blackline Masters 151–152

Children wear the story characters on **Blackline Masters 151–152** as they act out *The Three Little Pigs.* See page T63 for this week's Dramatic Play Center activity.

Art Center

VA.A.1.1.1

Materials • art paper • poster paints • feathers

Children paint with feathers, stroking with the soft end and drawing lines with the hard end. This technique works well for painting birds similar to those in *Feathers for Lunch.* See page T73 for this week's Art Center activity.

Book Center

SC.F.1.1.5

Materials • chart paper • crayons or markers • old magazines and catalogs

Children categorize animals by physical traits: feathers, fur, skin, scales, or shells. They color or cut out and label pictures of different animals, putting them where they belong on the category chart. See page T89 for this week's Science Center activity.

LA.B.2.1.2.K.1 writes with pictures, words
LA.E.2.1.1.K.2 uses personal interpretations
SC.F.1.1.5 characteristics of plants, animals

TH.A.1.1.1 uses basic acting skills
VA.A.1.1.1 uses 2-D, 3-D media

Day 1

Day at a Glance

Learning to Read

Read Aloud:

The Tale of the Three Little Pigs

✓ Reviewing / b /, / c /, / l /, page T66

Word Work

✓ High-Frequency Word Practice, page T68

Writing & Language

Oral Language, *page T69*

Opening

LA.A.2.1.5.K.2
★LA.A.1.1.2.K.6
★LA.A.1.1.3.K.4

Calendar

Sunday	Monday	Tuesday	Wednesday	Thursday	Friday	Saturday
			1	2	3	4
5	6	7	8	9	10	11
12	13	14	15	16	17	18
19	20	21	22	23	24	25
26	27	28	29	30	31	

Together, chant the months of the year. Then have children brainstorm words that rhyme with *spring* or the name of the current month.

Daily Message

Interactive Writing Today's message can be about animals that children have seen on a farm or in the neighborhood. As you write, ask volunteers to add the punctuation. Children can count the sentences, using end marks and capital letters at the beginning of a sentence as clues.

Katelyn saw three birds this morning. Ashley's dog got lost last night. She found him!

Call out a letter, and have children chant the spelling of each word that begins with that letter on the wall: **S! S-a-i-d** *spells* said *and* s-e-e *spells* see. T! t-o *spells* to *and* t-h-e *spells* the!

Routines

 ## Daily Phonemic Awareness
Blending and Segmenting Phonemes

- *I'm thinking of an animal. I'll say some sounds, and you put them together to guess my word: /p /... /ĭ /... /g /.* (pig). Continue, helping children blend sounds for *fish, cat, goat,* and *yak.*

- *Now I'll say a whole word. This time, you say each sound to your partner.* Say *bat,* stretching out the sounds. After partners confer, call on them to say the separate sounds. (/b/ /ă/ /t/) Continue with *hen, ant,* and *dog.*

Phoneme Substitution

Play "Pass the Word." Have children sit in a circle. Say the word *cat* and "pass" it to the next player. That child must change it into a new word by changing the beginning sound and passing the new word to the next player. Examples: *bat, chat, fat, hat, mat, gnat, pat, rat, sat, vat.* When no one can think of another word, switch to *hen* or *bug.*

 Sunshine State Standards pp. T60–T61
★ = FCAT Benchmark in Gr. 3–5

★**LA.A.1.1.2.K.5** basic phonetic principles
★**LA.A.1.1.2.K.6** print conveys meaning
★**LA.A.1.1.3.K.4** uses sources to build vocabulary
LA.A.2.1.5.K.2 pictures, signs for information
LA.C.1.1.4.K.1 listens for specific information

Getting Ready to Learn

To help plan their day, tell children that they will

- listen to a story called *The Tale of the Three Little Pigs.*

- visit with some Alphafriends: Benny Bear, Callie Cat, and Larry Lion.

- act out the story in the Dramatic Play Center.

Read Aloud

Purposes • oral language • listening strategy
• comprehension skill

Selection Summary
This classic folktale tells about three pigs who leave home and build their own houses. The pigs get into trouble, though, when a hungry wolf tries to catch them for his dinner.

Key Concepts
Important jobs are best done slowly and carefully.

English Language Learners

LA.A.1.1.1.K.1
Some of your English language learners may not be familiar with the story. While you are doing the Read Aloud, check for understanding. Ask them yes-no and choice questions to monitor comprehension. Encourage children to make predictions.

LA.C.1.1.1.K.1
LA.A.1.1.1.K.1
LA.C.1.1.1.K.2
LA.A.1.1.4.K.1
FCAT Benchmark in Gr. 3–5

Teacher Read Aloud
Oral Language/Comprehension

▶ **Building Background**

Tell children they're going to hear a story called *The Tale of the Three Little Pigs.* Ask who has heard it before. Talk about pigs, which are mentioned in the title. Then ask what children know about the other animal in the story—the wolf. Mention that in many old stories, the wolf plays tricks on the other characters.

Strategy: Predict/Infer

Teacher Modeling Model the Predict/Infer Strategy as you read the title and display the picture.

Think Aloud

I enjoy a story more when I predict, or figure out what might happen before I read it. I already know some things about pigs and about wolves in stories. Maybe this wolf will try to catch the pigs for his lunch! I'll read and see if my idea is the same as the author's. As you listen, you do that too.

✓ **Comprehension Focus: Compare and Contrast**

Teacher Modeling Model how to compare events or characters in a story.

Think Aloud

As I read, I'm going to ask myself what each pig does and how it is different from what the other pigs do. That will help me understand the story. You listen and think about the pigs too.

Sunshine State Standards pp. T62–T63   ★ = FCAT Benchmark in Gr. 3–5

LA.A.1.1.1.K.1 oral predictions   LA.C.1.1.1.K.2 listens to oral language
LA.A.1.1.4.K.1 strategies to comprehend text   TH.A.1.1.1 uses basic acting skills
LA.C.1.1.1.K.1 follows 2-step oral directions

▶ Listening to the Story

Add excitement to the story by using a gruff voice when you read the wolf's lines. Encourage children to chime in with the "huff-and-puff" refrain. Note that the Read Aloud art is available on the back of the Theme Poster.

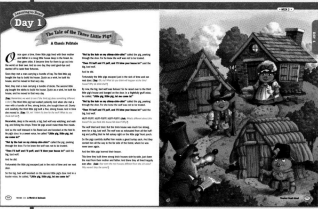

▶ Responding

Summarizing the Story Use these prompts to help children retell the story.

■ *What kind of houses did the pigs build at first? What happened to them?*

■ *How was the third little pig's house different?*

■ *Which pig had the best plan? Why? What lesson did the pigs learn?*

Practice Book pages 293–294 Children will complete the pages at small group time.

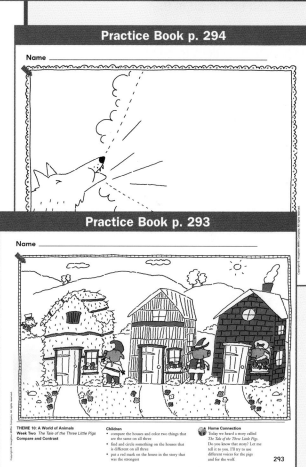

Practice Book p. 294

Practice Book p. 293

At Group Time
Dramatic Play Center

TH.A.1.1.1

Materials • Blackline Masters 151–152

Children can add features to the story characters on **Blackline Masters 151–152** and wear them as they act out the story. At the end, characters can tell what they learned from the third little pig.

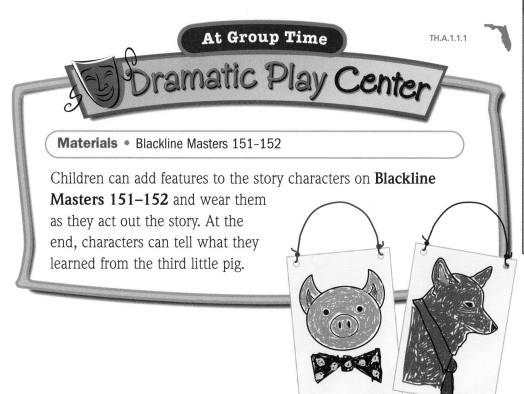

Teacher's Note

Read Aloud Tip Read another story of three, such as *Goldilocks and the Three Bears* or *The Three Billy Goats Gruff.* Discuss what is the same and different in those stories.

The Tale of the Three Little Pigs

A Classic Folktale

Once upon a time, three little pigs lived with their mother and father in a snug little house deep in the forest. As they grew older, it became time for them to go out into the world on their own. And so one day, they said good-bye and started off to seek their fortunes.

Soon they met a man carrying a bundle of hay. The first little pig bought the hay to build his house. Quick as a wink, he built his house, and he moved in that very day.

Next, they met a man carrying a bundle of sticks. The second little pig bought the sticks to build his house. Quick as a wink, he built his house, and he moved in that very day.

(**Say:** *Remember, we want to see if the third pig does something different. Listen.*) The third little pig had waited patiently. And when she met a man with a bundle of fine, strong bricks, she bought them all. Slowly and carefully, the third little pig built a fine, strong house. And in time she moved in. (**Say:** *Oh, no! I think it's time for the wolf! What do you think he'll do?*)

Meanwhile, deep in the woods, a big, bad wolf was watching, and waiting, and licking his chops. Three fat pigs would make three fine meals.

And so the wolf dressed in his finest suit and knocked at the first little pig's door. In a sweet voice, he called **"Little pig, little pig, let me come in!"**

"Not by the hair on my chinny-chin-chin!" called the pig, peeking through the door. For he knew the wolf was not to be trusted.

"Then I'll huff and I'll puff, and I'll blow your house in!" said the big, bad wolf.

And he did.

Fortunately the little pig escaped just in the nick of time and ran next door.

So the big, bad wolf knocked on the second little pig's door. And in a louder voice, he called, **"Little pig, little pig, let me come in!"**

"Not by the hair on my chinny-chin-chin!" called the pig, peeking through the door. For he knew the wolf was not to be trusted.

"Then I'll huff and I'll puff, and I'll blow your house in!" said the big, bad wolf.

And he did.

Fortunately the little pigs escaped just in the nick of time and ran next door. (**Say:** *Oh, my! What do you think will happen at the third house? Why do think that?*)

By now, the big, bad wolf was furious! So he raced over to the third little pig's house and banged on the door. In a frightfully gruff voice, he called, **"Little pig, little pig, let me come in!"**

"Not by the hair on my chinny-chin-chin!" called the pig, peeking through the door. For she knew the wolf was not to be trusted.

"Then I'll huff and I'll puff, and I'll blow your house in!" said the big, bad wolf.

HUFF-PUFF! HUFF-PUFF! HUFF-PUFF! (**Ask:** *What's different about this house? Do you think this house fell down? Why?*)

The wolf tried and tried. But the brick house was much too strong, even for a big, bad wolf. The wolf was so exhausted from all the huffing and puffing that he fell asleep right on the little pigs' front porch.

So the pigs carefully stuffed him inside a great burlap sack. And they carried him all the way to the far side of the forest, where he was never seen again.

And the little pigs learned their lesson.

This time they built three strong brick houses side-by-side, just down the road from their mother and father. And there they all lived happily ever after. (**Ask:** *How were the new houses different from the old ones? Why weren't they the same?*)

Teacher Read Aloud

Learning to Read
Day 1

Home Connection

For parents who would like to review the Alphafriends' songs with their children, take-home versions are on **Alphafriends Blackline Masters.**

English Language Learners

★LA.A.1.1.2.K.3

The sounds of /p/ and /b/ are not plosive in some languages. Exaggerate this characteristic, having English language learners put their hands in front of their mouths to feel the air coming out when they say these sounds. As needed, demonstrate how to position the lips.

Phonemic Awareness
✓ Initial Sounds

▶ Alphafriend: Benny Bear

This week we'll review some of our old Alphafriends. Use this routine to review Benny Bear.

1 **Alphafriend Riddle** Read these clues:

- *This Alphafriend's sound is /b/. Say it with me: /b/.*
- *This big beast is named Benny.*

When most hands are up, call on children until they guess *bear.*

2 **Pocket Chart** Display Benny Bear in a pocket chart. Say his name, emphasizing the /b/ sound slightly, and have children echo the sound.

3 📼 **Alphafriend Audiotape** Play Benny Bear's song, or read it from the **Alphafriends Blackline Master.** *Listen for words that begin with /b/.*

4 **Alphafolder** Have children look at the scene and name the /b/ pictures.

5 **Summarize**

- *What is our Alphafriend's name? What is his sound?*
- Display the Picture Cards. *Which pictures start like Benny's name? Put those cards in the chart next to Benny.*
- *Each time you look at Benny Bear this week, remember the /b/ sound.*

6 Repeat this routine for Larry Lion and Callie Cat. Use the clues below.

- for Larry: *This animal likes to leap.*
- for Callie: *This furry character curls up in a ball.*

Bennie Bear's Song
(tune: Three Blind Mice)

Benny Bear, Benny Bear.
Please beware! Please beware!
I see a bee near the basket
   of beets.
The bee is buzzing by
   buttery treats.
Please don't run. Eat
   your bun!

▶ Listening for /b/, /k/, /l/

Compare and Review Display the three Alphafriends. Tell children you'll name some pictures. For each one, children should think of the Alphafriend whose name begins with the same sound. Ask a volunteer to put the Picture Card below the correct Alphafriend.

Pictures: *bell, bike, bug, can, cow, cot, lamp, leaf, lock*

Tell children that they will sort more pictures in the Phonics Center today.

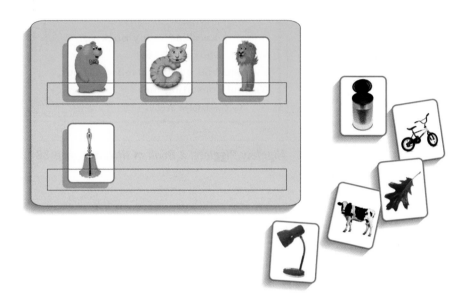

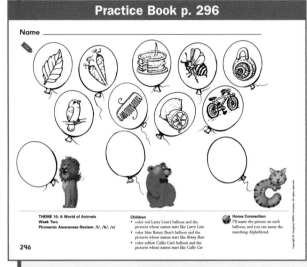

Practice Book p. 296

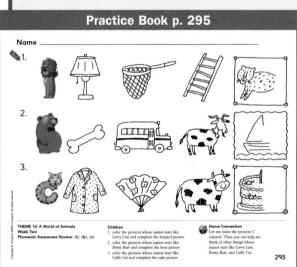

Practice Book p. 295

▶ Apply

Practice Book pages 295–296 Children will complete the pages at small group time.

At Group Time

Phonics Center

*LA.A.1.1.2.K.2, 3, 5

Use the Phonics Center materials for **Theme 10, Week 2, Day 1**.

Day 1

★LA.A.1.1.3.K.1
LA.B.2.1.1.K.2

High-Frequency Word Practice

▶ Matching Words

■ Display cards for the high-frequency words *I, a, the, said, it, for, my,* and *see* in a pocket chart. Call on children to identify each word and to find its match on the Word Wall.

■ Distribute the cards. Then read the poem "Tommy" line by line, and have children match the Word Cards to the same words in the poem.

Tommy

I put a seed into the ground
And said, "I'll watch it grow."
I watered it and cared for it
As well as I could know.

One day I walked in my back yard,
And oh, what did I see!
My seed had popped itself right out,
Without consulting me.

by Gwendolyn Brooks

38

Higglety Pigglety: A Book of Rhymes, page 38

Teacher's Note

You will need a word card for *an* to build some of the sentences.

Writing Opportunity In the pocket chart place the Word Cards *She and I go to see a* _____ . Tell children to pretend that one of the three little pigs is speaking about his sister. Read the sentence together. Children can use Picture Cards, such as *ant, horse, house,* and *man,* to finish it in different ways. Provide an alternate sentence using *an* instead of *a,* and mention the use of *an* before words that begin with vowel sounds.

Later, children can copy the sentences and complete them with their own drawings.

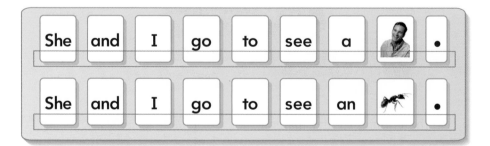

Sunshine State Standards pp. T68–T69   ★ = FCAT Benchmark in Gr. 3–5

★**LA.A.1.1.3.K.1** identifies high-frequency words   **LA.B.2.1.2.K.1** writes with pictures, words
LA.B.2.1.1.K.2 ideas to shared writing   **LA.D.2.1.2.K.1** uses repetition, rhyme in texts

Oral Language

▶ Using Rhyming Words

■ Talk about rhyming words with children. Remind them that short rhyming words have the same middle and ending sounds, as in *cut/hut, wet/set,* and *skate/gate.* Ask volunteers to name some other rhyming pairs.

■ Tell children you will name words from *The Tale of the Three Little Pigs* and they should think of words that rhyme with each one. As you name each word, draw a simple picture of it on a chart. Then list children's ideas below it.

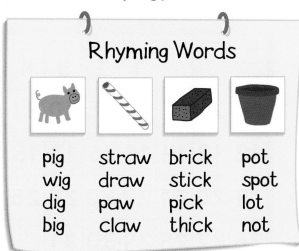

Rhyming Words

pig	straw	brick	pot
wig	draw	stick	spot
dig	paw	pick	lot
big	claw	thick	not

LA.D.2.1.2.K.1
LA.B.2.1.2.K.1

At Group Time

Put the chart in the Writing Center. Partners can refer to the pictures to help them read the rhyming lists. Together, they can think of a scene that includes two things whose names rhyme, draw a picture, and add a caption. Collect the pages for a class book of rhymes.

Mouse in a house.

OBJECTIVES

Children
● use rhyming words

 Portfolio Opportunity

Have children write their names on pages they contribute to the class book of rhymes. When parents come in for conference time, share their child's page as a drawing and writing sample.

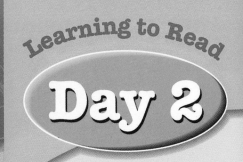
Day at a Glance

Learning to Read

Big Book:

Feathers for Lunch

✓ **Phonics: Initial Consonants** *b, c, l, page T74*

✓ **High-Frequency Word** *he, page T76*

Word Work

High-Frequency Word Practice, *page T78*

Writing & Language

Vocabulary Expansion, *page T79*

Opening

LA.A.2.1.5.K.2
★LA.A.1.1.2.K.6
★LA.A.1.1.3.K.4

Calendar

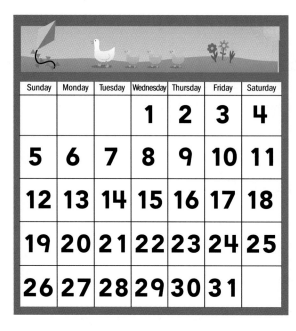

Sunday	Monday	Tuesday	Wednesday	Thursday	Friday	Saturday
			1	2	3	4
5	6	7	8	9	10	11
12	13	14	15	16	17	18
19	20	21	22	23	24	25
26	27	28	29	30	31	

Together, spell this month's name. Ask if anyone in the class has a first or last name that begins with the same letter as this month's name.

Daily Message

Modeled Writing Use some rhyming words in today's message. After reading the message, ask children which two words rhyme. Circle those words.

Mr. Brown can help us get a new pet for our room .

Play "Pass the Pointer." Say a word and have a child find it with a pointer. That child then says another word from the wall and passes the pointer to the next player, who must find the word. Continue until everyone plays.

Routines

✓ Daily Phonemic Awareness
Blending and Segmenting Phonemes

Play a wolf-code game. *I'll be the first little pig. You can be my family. When you knock, I'll ask a special question. If you know the answer, I'll be sure you are not the wolf and I can open the door.* Have children "knock" on a table or the floor. *What is the code word? The sounds are /p/... /i/... /g/.*

Sunshine State Standards pp. T70–T71
★ = FCAT Benchmark in Gr. 3–5

★**LA.A.1.1.2.K.5** basic phonetic principles
★**LA.A.1.1.2.K.6** print conveys meaning
★**LA.A.1.1.3.K.4** uses sources to build vocabulary
LA.A.2.1.5.K.2 pictures, signs for information
LA.C.1.1.4.K.1 listens for specific information

- Have partners confer and raise their hands when they have blended the sounds. When most hands are up, have children say the word together and then "open the door" for them. Continue with *cat, dog,* and *kit.* Then change the game so that you say the whole word and partners say the separate sounds.

✓ Phoneme Substitution

Play another game. Say *pig* and its three separate sounds. Explain that you want to change the last sound to /n/. *Listen: /p/ /ĭ/ /g/ changes to /p/ /ĭ/ /n/. What's the new word?* (pin) Continue, helping children substitute final /n/ for /t/ in *cat* (can), final /t/ for /g/ in *dog* (dot); final /s/ for /t/ in *kit* (kiss).

Getting Ready to Learn

To help plan their day, tell children that they will

- listen to a Big Book: *Feathers for Lunch.*

- review the letters *Bb, Cc,* and *Ll* and their sounds.

- act out their new story *Feathers for Lunch* in the Dramatic Play Center.

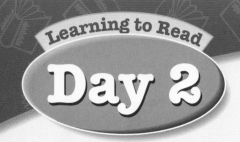

Learning to Read
Day 2

Big Book

HOUGHTON MIFFLIN Reading

Feathers for Lunch

Lois Ehlert

Includes: Science Link

Purposes • concepts of print • story language • reading strategy • comprehension skill

---

Selection Summary
Follow a hungry cat and learn about birds in this humorous, rhyming story.

Key Concepts
Types of birds and their calls
Bird homes and food

MEETING INDIVIDUAL NEEDS

English Language Learners

LA.C.2.1.1.K.1

Before reading, preview the pictures of the birds. Guide them with questions about color, size, shape, of the beak, and so on. Have a bell to ring when you read the story. Explain how the cat's bell warns the birds away.

Sharing the Big Book
Oral Language/Comprehension

▶ Building Background

Introduce the Big Book by reading the title and the name of the author/illustrator. Ask children what they know about birds. You add to the discussion too, sharing a few facts about your favorite birds. *Are all birds the same? Name some places where birds live. What kinds of food do they eat? What do birds sound like? What animals like to eat them?*

Strategy: Predict/Infer

Teacher Modeling Model how to use the title and the cover to help you predict what the selection is about.

> **Think Aloud**
>
> *Before I read a book, I think about the title and the cover, and I guess what the book may be about. The word* feathers *is in the title. Birds have feathers, so maybe this book has birds in it. But feathers aren't good to eat, so* Feathers for Lunch *is a strange title. Maybe this book has a funny ending.*

✓ Comprehension Focus: Compare and Contrast

Teacher Modeling Do a brief picture walk through page 11. Model how to compare and contrast as you read.

> **Think Aloud**
>
> *As I read, I'll think about how things are the same and how they are different. I notice a lot of birds in this book. They all have feathers, but they are not all the same. They are shown in different places, and they are eating different things. Noticing these things will help me learn about birds.*

Sunshine State Standards pp. T72–T73   ★ = FCAT Benchmark in Gr. 3–5

LA.A.1.1.1.K.1 oral predictions
LA.C.1.1.1.K.2 listens to oral language
LA.C.2.1.1.K.1 main idea in nonprint

LA.E.2.1.1.K.2 uses personal interpretations
LA.E.2.1.2.K.1 knows rhymes in text
SC.F.1.1.5 characteristics of plants, animals

▶ Sharing the Story

As you read the selection, emphasize the rhyming words. Pause to prompt children to notice different birds and what they do.

▶ Responding

Personal Response Have children tell what they liked about the story.

- *Which pages did you like best? Which birds were your favorites?*

- *Did anything happen that you guessed from the title and the picture on the cover? Why did the cat get feathers for lunch?*

- *Have you seen any real birds that look just like these? What other birds do you know?*

Page through the book, pointing out the names of the birds and inviting children to repeat their calls with you.

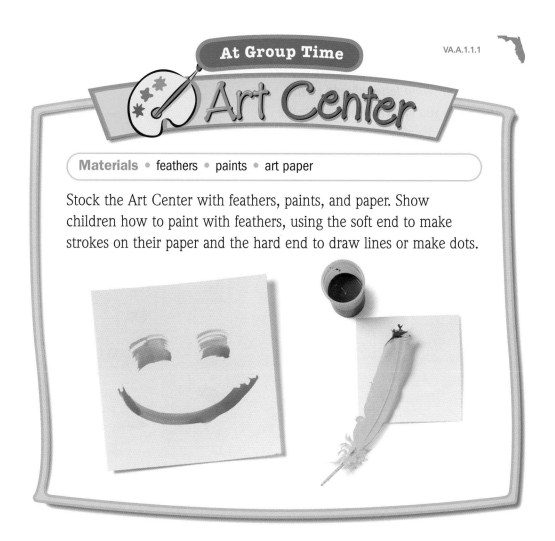

At Group Time

VA.A.1.1.1

Art Center

Materials • feathers • paints • art paper

Stock the Art Center with feathers, paints, and paper. Show children how to paint with feathers, using the soft end to make strokes on their paper and the hard end to draw lines or make dots.

MEETING INDIVIDUAL NEEDS

Extra Support

SC.F.1.1.5

Take out several picture books on birds from the library. Choose one characteristic of birds, such as coloring. Then page through the books with children, discussing how that feature is the same or different in various kinds of birds.

VA.A.1.1.1 uses 2-D, 3-D media

Learning to Read
Day 2

Phonics

✓ Reviewing Initial Consonants b, c, l

▶ Develop Phonemic Awareness

Beginning Sounds Read aloud the lyrics from Benny Bear's song and have children echo it line for line. Have them listen for the /b/ words and *bounce* for each one. Repeat for /k/ and /l/ with *Callie Cat* and *Larry Lion,* having children *clap* or *laugh* for each target word.

▶ Connect Sounds to Letters

Beginning Letters Display *Benny Bear* and have children name the letter on the picture. *What letter stands for the sound /b/, as in* bear? *Which animal will help you remember the sound for* b?

Repeat this routine with *Larry Lion* and *Callie Cat.*

Now tell children you want to write *bake* on the board. *What letter should I write first? How do you know?* Repeat with the words *lake* and *cake.*

Compare and Review: *b, c, l* In the pocket chart, display the Letter Cards as shown and the Picture Cards in random order. In turn, children can name a picture, say the beginning sound, and put the card below the right letter.

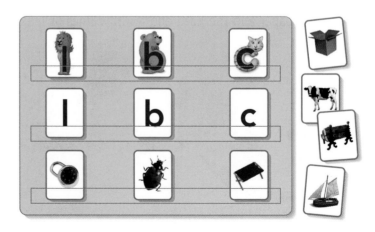

Sunshine State Standards pp. T74–T75   ★ = FCAT Benchmark in Gr. 3–5

★**LA.A.1.1.2.K.2** knows alphabet
★**LA.A.1.1.2.K.3** knows sounds of alphabet
★**LA.A.1.1.2.K.5** basic phonetic principles

▶ Handwriting

Writing *B*, *b*, *C*, *c*, *L*, *l* Tell children that now they'll practice writing the letters that stand for /b/: capital *B* and small *b*. Ask children to write each letter in the air as you recite the handwriting rhyme together. Review *C*, *c*, *L*, and *l* in the same way.

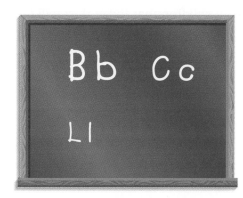

▶ Apply

Practice Book page 297 Children can complete this page at small group time.

Blackline Masters 158, 159, 168 These pages provide additional handwriting practice for small group time.

Practice Book p. 297

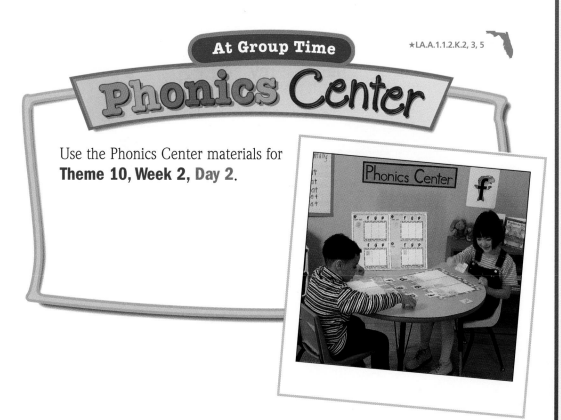

At Group Time
Phonics Center

★LA.A.1.1.2.K.2, 3, 5

Use the Phonics Center materials for **Theme 10, Week 2, Day 2**.

Teacher's Note

Handwriting practice for the continuous stroke style is available on **Blackline Masters 184, 185, 194.**

Portfolio Opportunity

Save the **Practice Book** page to show children's grasp of the letter-sound associations.

Save **Blackline Masters 158, 159, 168** for handwriting samples.

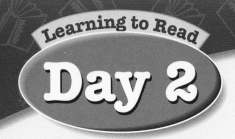

Learning to Read
Day 2

Children

• read and write the high-frequency word *he*

MATERIALS

• **Word Cards** *he, He, here, is, Is, my*

• **Picture Card** *dog*

• **Punctuation Cards:** period, question mark

• **Big Book:** *Feathers for Lunch*

✓ High-Frequency Word

New Word: he

▶ Teach

Tell children that today they will learn to read and write a word that they will often see in stories. Say *he* and use it in context.

> *He* is hungry.   *He* and I watched the birds.   I thought *he* was here.

Write *he* on the board, and have children spell it as you point to the letters. Say, **Spell he with me,** **h-e.** Then lead children in a chant, clapping on each beat, to help them remember the letters in *he:* **h-e, he! h-e, he!**

Word Wall   Post *he* on the Word Wall, and remind children to look there when they need to remember how to write the word.

▶ Practice

Reading Build sentences in a pocket chart as shown. Children can take turns reading. Then place the pocket chart in the **Phonics Center** so that children can practice building and reading sentences.

English Language Learners

★LA.A.1.1.2.K.3

Remind children that in English the letter *h* has the sound /h/. Have them practice /h/ as a beginning sound, making sure they can feel the air coming out of their mouth. Introduce the word *he* as part of the phonemic practice. Then help English language learners practice using *he* and *she* by referring to classmates as *he* or *she*.

Sunshine State Standards pp. T76–T77   ★ = FCAT Benchmark in Gr. 3–5

★LA.A.1.1.2.K.3 knows sounds of alphabet
★LA.A.1.1.3.K.1 identifies high-frequency words
★LA.A.1.1.3.K.4 uses sources to build vocabulary

Display the Big Book *Feathers for Lunch,* page 3.

■ Reread the page slowly, tracking the print. Have children point to the word *he* when it appears.

■ Leaf slowly through the pages of the book, encouraging children to notice and point to the word *he.* Remind them to look for the word *He* with a capital *H* also.

▶ Apply

Practice Book page 298 Children will read and write *he* as they complete the Practice Book page. On Day 3, they will practice reading *he* in the **Phonics Library** story "It Can Fit."

Practice Book p. 298

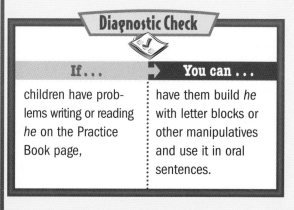

Diagnostic Check

If...	➤ You can...
children have problems writing or reading *he* on the Practice Book page,	have them build *he* with letter blocks or other manipulatives and use it in oral sentences.

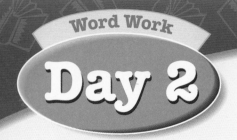

Day 2

★LA.A.1.1.3.K.1
LA.B.1.1.3.K.2

High-Frequency Word Practice

➤ Building Sentences

Tell children that you want to build a sentence about sharing a pet.

- Display the Word Cards and Picture Cards in random order. Take the word *He*, put it in the pocket chart, and read it.

- *I will leave a space next to the word* **He.**

- *I want the next word to be* **and.** *Who can find that word?*

- Continue building *He and I have a cat.* Read the completed sentence together.

- Scramble the cards and have volunteers build and read the sentence several times. Children can choose different Picture Cards to replace *cat.*

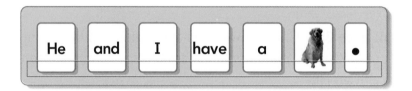

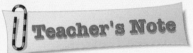 **Writing Opportunity** Suggest that children write their own sentences about pets and illustrate them. Children might use the displayed sentence as a model. Remind children to use temporary phonics spellings by saying words slowly and writing the letters they hear.

He is my cat Max.

OBJECTIVES

Children

- read high-frequency words
- create and write sentences with high-frequency words

MATERIALS

- **Word Cards** *a, and, have, He, I, is, my*
- **Picture Cards** *dog, fish* and other animals you choose
- **Punctuation Card:** period

Teacher's Note

Prepare the word card *cat* for this activity.

Sunshine State Standards pp. T78–T79　　★ = FCAT Benchmark in Gr. 3–5

★**LA.A.1.1.2.K.5** basic phonetic principles　　LA.B.1.1.3.K.2 directionality of print
★**LA.A.1.1.3.K.1** identifies high-frequency words　　LA.B.2.1.1.K.2 ideas to shared writing
★**LA.A.1.1.3.K.2** identifies noun words

Vocabulary Expansion

★LA.A.1.1.2.K.5
★LA.A.1.1.3.K.2
LA.B.2.1.1.K.2

▶ Using Exact Words, Rhyming Words

Write *bird* on the board and read it. Point out that *bird* is a general word—it could mean *any* bird. Explain that the author of *Feathers for Lunch* made her book more interesting by using *exact* naming words for special types of birds.

Listening and Viewing Page through *Feathers for Lunch*, pointing to the labels next to the birds in the art. Read these exact words and have children describe the birds they name. Ask, for example: **When you hear the word** robin *in a story, what color bird will you think of?*

Remind children that *Feathers for Lunch* also includes many rhyming words. Read verses from the story, and have children name the rhyming pairs. Extend the activity by saying the name of a bird and asking children to think of rhymes.

 Writing Opportunity Use the exact words and naming words from the activity to build some descriptive sentences.

- On chart paper, write *I see a _____ in a _____.* Read it to children.

- Model making a rhyming sentence: *Let's add the word* wren. *Now we have* I see a wren in a _____. *What rhymes with* wren? pen? *Let's write* I see a wren in a pen.

- Write the ideas children suggest. They can be as real or as fanciful as children wish.

I see a wren in a pen.

I see a jay on the hay.

I see a parrot on a carrot.

OBJECTIVES

Children

- use exact naming words
- use rhyming words

MATERIALS

- **Big Book:** *Feathers for Lunch*

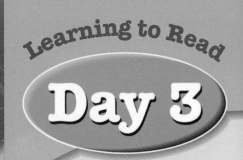

Learning to Read

Day 3

Day at a Glance

Learning to Read

Big Book:

Feathers for Lunch

☑ **Phonics:**
Blending
c, -ut,
page T90

Word Work

Building Words, *page T92*

Writing & Language

Shared Writing, *page T93*

Managing Small Groups

Teacher-Led Group
- Read **Phonics Library** selection "It Can Fit"
- Write letters *U, u; begin* **Blackline Masters 177 or 203.**
- Begin *Practice Book, 299–300*

Independent Groups
- Finish **Blackline Masters 177 or 203** and *Practice Book, 299–300*
- Math, Science, other Centers

Opening

LA.A.2.1.5.K.2
★LA.A.1.1.2.K.6
★LA.A.1.1.3.K.4

Calendar

Sunday	Monday	Tuesday	Wednesday	Thursday	Friday	Saturday
			1	2	3	4
5	6	7	8	9	10	11
12	13	14	15	16	17	18
19	20	21	22	23	24	25
26	27	28	29	30	31	

Point to and read the day and date on the calendar. Mention a well-known saying about this month, such as "the merry month of May" or "a lazy day in June," and discuss it. Have children close their eyes, and then ask them what letter is at the beginning of this month's name. Ask how they knew.

Daily Message

Interactive Writing Before writing the daily message, tell children what you want it to say. Name each letter and word as you write, stressing that writing is speech written down. Occasionally have volunteers write an initial consonant or a known word. Point out capital letters and end punctuation.

Today we will look at birds.

Choose a volunteer to point to and read the word that was added this week. (he) **What other h words are on the wall?** Continue reading the remaining groups of words.

Routines

✓ Daily Phonemic Awareness
Blending and Segmenting Phonemes

Read "Quack! Quack! Quack!" on page 29 of *Higglety Pigglety*. Explain that children will be birds, flapping for each sound and hopping when they say the word: flap, flap, flap, hop.

- Demonstrate with the word *big*. Have children perform the actions (flap, flap, flap, hop) with you. Help children hear and blend the sounds. Continue with *duck* and *but*.

- Play the same game, segmenting the words this time. Reverse the hopping and flapping: *big* (hop), / b / (flap), / ĭ / (flap), / g / (flap). Continue with *duck* and *but*.

✓ Phoneme Substitution

- Help children substitute final /l/ for /g/ in *big* to make the new word *bill*. Then have them substitute /g/ for /k/ in *duck* to make the new word *dug* and /d/ for /t/ in *but* to make *bud*.

Sunshine State Standards pp. T80–T81
★ = FCAT Benchmark in Gr. 3–5

★**LA.A.1.1.2.K.5** basic phonetic principles
★**LA.A.1.1.2.K.6** print conveys meaning
★**LA.A.1.1.3.K.4** uses sources to build vocabulary
LA.A.2.1.5.K.2 pictures, signs for information
LA.C.1.1.4.K.1 listens for specific information

DAY 3

Getting Ready to Learn

To help plan their day, tell children that they will

- reread and talk about the Big Book *Feathers for Lunch*.

- read a story called "It Can Fit."

It Can Fit
by Thomas Alexander
illustrated by Bernadette Pons

- classify in the Science Center.

feathers

skin

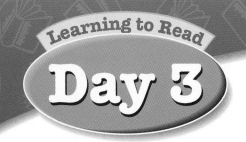

Learning to Read
Day 3

Sharing the Big Book

LA.C.1.1.1.K.2
LA.E.2.1.2.K.1

OBJECTIVES

Children

- compare and contrast elements in a story
- identify the end of a sentence and the ending punctuation

Big Book
Reading

Feathers for Lunch

Lois Ehlert

Includes:
Science Link

Reading for Understanding Reread the story, emphasizing the rhyme and rhythm. Pause for discussion points.

Extra Support

★LA.A.1.1.2.K.4

Make three cards showing a period, a question mark, and an exclamation point. Ask children to shrug (as if asking a question) when you show the question mark, throw their hands in the air when they see an exclamation point, and stand still for the period.

Uh-oh.
Door's left open,
just a crack.

title, page 1

My cat is out
and he won't
come back!

geranium
plant

pages 2–3

JINGLE
JINGLE

American Robin

He's looking for lunch,
something new,

TOMATO

pages 4–5

Sunshine State Standards pp. T82–T83   ★ = FCAT Benchmark in Gr. 3–5

★**LA.A.1.1.2.K.4** concept of words, meaning   **LA.C.1.1.1.K.2** listens to oral language
★**LA.A.2.1.1.K.1** main idea from a read-aloud   **LA.E.2.1.2.K.1** knows rhymes in text
LA.A.1.1.1.K.1 oral predictions

a spicy treat for today's menu.

pages 6–7

His food in a can is tame and mild,

pages 8–9

so he's gone out for something wild.

pages 10–11

▶ Supporting Comprehension

title page
Strategy: Predict/Infer ^{LA.A.1.1.1.K.1}

Teacher-Student Modeling Talk about how you made predictions about the story before reading yesterday. Prompts:

- *What clues did the title and pictures give us? Did the story have birds in it?*

pages 4–5 ★LA.A.2.1.1.K.1
Drawing Conclusions

- *What does the cat in this picture want for lunch?* (something new for lunch, a bird)

pages 8–9 ★LA.A.2.1.1.K.1
Noting Details

- *What do you notice around the cat's neck?* (There's a collar with a tag and a bell on it.) **Point to the words *jingle jingle*. *These words show that the bell keeps jingling throughout the book.***

pages 8–11
Comprehension Focus: _{FCAT Benchmark in Gr. 3–5}
Compare and Contrast

Teacher-Student Modeling Remind children to watch for what's the same and what's different in the story. *How is being fed food from a can different from what this cat is doing?* (The canned food is "tame," and this cat wants to hunt for "something wild.")

Oral Language
On a rereading, note the author's use of interesting words, bird names, birdcalls, and plant names.

Vocabulary
tame: *Tame* means "easy to control; no longer wild."
mild: *Mild* means "gentle; not harsh."

DAY 3

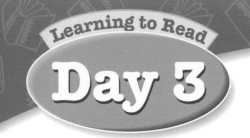
▶ Supporting Comprehension

pages 12–13

- -

page 12–17

Comprehension Focus: FCAT Benchmark in Gr. 3–5
Compare and Contrast

Teacher-Student Modeling *How are the birds on these pages the same?* (They all have feathers, tails, wings, and beaks.) *How are they different?* (Their colors, their beaks, and the places they like to perch are different.)

pages 14–15   LA.A.2.1.4.K.1

Fantasy/Realism

■ *Could this story really happen? What makes you think so?* (Yes, because cats really do chase birds, and birds call and warn each other.)

pages 16–17   ★LA.A.2.1.1.K.1

Noting Details

■ *Look at the bird on this page. What do you notice about its body? What is it doing? Where is it perched?* (It's perched on the edge of the lilac bush, ready to fly away.)

pages 16–17   FCAT Benchmark in Gr. 3–5

Cause and Effect

■ *What happens every time the cat's bell jingles?* (The birds hear the bell jingle, call to warn each other, and fly away.)

pages 14–15

pages 16–17

Sunshine State Standards pp. T84–T85   ★ = FCAT Benchmark in Gr. 3–5

★**LA.A.1.1.3.K.4** uses sources to build vocabulary   **LA.A.2.1.4.K.1** illustrations reinforce text
★**LA.A.1.1.3.K.5** develops vocabulary   **LA.C.2.1.1.K.1** main idea in nonprint
★**LA.A.2.1.1.K.1** main idea from a read-aloud

pages 18–19

pages 20–21

pages 22–23

▶ Supporting Comprehension

pages 20–21 LA.C.2.1.1.K.1
Drawing Conclusions

■ *Look at the picture. Where do these birds live?*

(in a hole in a tree)

pages 22–23 ★LA.A.1.1.3.K.5
Making Judgments

■ *What does the author mean when she writes "birds know what their wings are for"? What will wings help this bird do?* (get away from the cat)

---

pages 20–23

Comprehension Focus: FCAT Benchmark in Gr. 3–5
Compare and Contrast

Student Modeling Discuss the ways cats and birds move around.

■ *How do cats move from place to place? How do they prowl? How do cats get into trees and high places?*

■ *How do birds move around on the ground? in the air?*

■ Call on volunteers to tell how the cat compares to the bird on these pages in size, body traits, and movements.

MEETING INDIVIDUAL NEEDS

Challenge

★LA.A.1.1.3.K.4

Some children will be able to find words from the Word Wall, such as *and, for, he, is,* and *my* in the story.

DAY 3

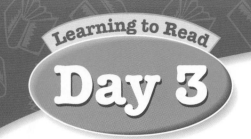
▶ Supporting Comprehension

pages 26–27 LA.C.2.1.1.K.1

Drawing Conclusions

- *What is happening in this picture? Did the cat ever catch a bird?* (The cat has been caught by a person. He didn't catch a bird.)

pages 26–27

Strategy: Predict/Infer LA.A.1.1.1.K.1

Student Modeling *Do you think this cat will ever be able to catch one of the birds? Do you think the cat will ever stop chasing birds? Explain.* Help children use what they learned from the story and what they know about birds in real life to discuss a variety of different answers.

Rhyme Reread appropriate sentences from the book, pausing for children to supply the final rhyming word.

Challenge

LA.C.2.1.1.K.1
★LA.A.1.1.3.K.5

Help children understand that the cat almost caught the bird. Say: *Look at the art. Why does the cat have feathers in his mouth? Did he catch the bird or almost catch the bird?* Help children to understand that *caught* is the past of *catch.*

pages 24–25

pages 26–27

pages 28–29

Sunshine State Standards pp. T86–T87   ★ = FCAT Benchmark in Gr. 3–5

★LA.A.1.1.2.K.4 concept of words, meaning   LA.A.1.1.1.K.1 oral predictions
★LA.A.1.1.3.K.5 develops vocabulary   LA.C.2.1.1.K.1 main idea in nonprint
★LA.A.2.1.1.K.1 main idea from a read-aloud

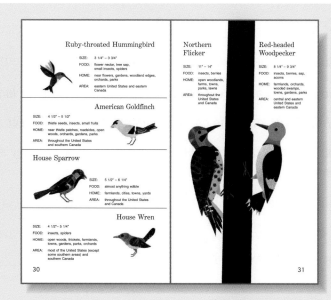

pages 30–31

 **Supporting Comprehension**

pages 28–31 ★LA.A.2.1.1.K.1

Noting Details

■ Point out that each bird on these pages is also shown in the book. Read the information about each bird, and have children find it in the story. Encourage children to describe the birds in detail.

Revisiting the Text

pages 8–27

Concepts of Print ★LA.A.1.1.2.K.4

 End of Sentence/End Punctuation

■ Track the print slowly on pages 8–27 as you read it aloud again. Tell children to chirp like a bird when you come to an end punctuation mark, indicating where to stop.

DAY 3

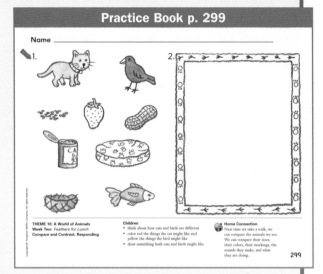

Practice Book p. 299

Name _____

THEME 10: A World of Animals
Week Two *Feathers for Lunch*
Compare and Contrast, Responding

Children
• think about how cats and birds are different
• color red the things the cat might like and yellow the things the bird might like
• draw something both cats and birds might like

Home Connection
Next time we take a walk, we can compare the animals we see. We can compare their uses, their colors, their markings, the sounds they make, and what they are doing.

299

▶ ## Responding to the Story
LA.A.1.1.4.K.1

Summarizing Use these prompts to help children summarize the selection:

■ *What did the cat want to eat? What did it end up having for lunch?*

■ *How did the birds know the cat was coming? How did they get away?*

■ *Tell about two of your favorite birds in the book. How are they alike? How are they different?*

Practice Book page 299 Children will complete the page at small group time.

Literature Circle Have small groups discuss the story. Then have children take turns acting out their favorite parts of the story with a partner.

Diagnostic Check

If...	You can...
children need help in remembering the concepts *same* and *different,*	have partners take turns noticing something that is the same about each other, and something that is different.

Sunshine State Standards pp. T88–T89   ★ = FCAT Benchmark in Gr. 3–5

★**LA.A.1.1.3.K.4** uses sources to build vocabulary
LA.A.1.1.4.K.1 strategies to comprehend text
SC.F.1.1.5 characteristics of plants, animals

At Group Time

SC.F.1.1.5

± = Math Center

Together, look through magazines for photographs of birds. Talk with children about the different characteristics of birds, including coloring, body traits, and habitats. Point out, for example, that some birds have tufts, while others do not; some birds live in water, some on land. Have children help you sort the pictures into categories they name.

At Group Time

SC.F.1.1.5

Science Center

Explain to children that birds are the only animals that have feathers. Other kinds of animals have other kinds of body coverings, such as fur, skin, scales, and shells. Start an animal category chart with sample pictures, and post it in the Science Center. Children can look through books and magazines to find pictures of animals that fit into each category. They can draw or cut out from magazines pictures of the animals and paste them in the right places. Help children label the pictures.

English Language Learners

★LA.A.1.1.3.K.4

Children will be able to collect and sort pictures for the Center activities, but may need support with vocabulary that describes animal features. Pair English language learners with fluent speakers for shared learning experience.

DAY 3

Learning to Read
Day 3

Practice Book p. 300

Name _____

| cut hut but |

Can you _____ a pan?
☺ ☹

Nan can go, _____ I can not.
☺ ☹

She ran to a _____ .
☺ ☹

THEME 10: A World of Animals
Week Two
Phonics: *b, c, -ut*

Children
• read the questions and write *cut, hut,* and *but* to complete them
• mark the smile (yes) or the frown (no) to show their answers to the sentences

Home Connection
Let's write *cut, hut,* and *but* on separate scraps of paper. Then we can turn the words face down and take turns picking one and making up a sentence with that word.

300

MEETING INDIVIDUAL NEEDS

Extra Support

★LA.A.1.1.2.K.3, 5

With children, make a list of words that begin with the short *u* sound *(umbrella, umpire, up, under).* Draw a simple picture next to each word to show its meaning. Read each word, pointing to each letter, and emphasize the short *u* sound.

Phonics

✓ *Blending* c *-ut*

▶ **Connect Sounds to Letters**

Review Consonant *c* Play Callie Cat's song, and have children clap for each /k/ word. Write *C* and *c* on the board, and list words from the song.

Blending *-ut* Tell children that they'll build a word with *c,* but first they'll review a vowel ("helper letter"). Display Alphafriend *Umbie Umbrella.*

This character is an umbrella. Say **Umbie Umbrella** *with me. Umbie's letter is the vowel* u, *and one sound that* u *stands for is* /ŭ/. Hold up Letter Card *u. Say* /ŭ/. *Listen for* /ŭ/ *in these words:* /ŭ/us, /ŭ/under, /ŭ/up.

Hold up the Letter Cards *c, u,* and *t.* Remind children that they know all the letters and sounds they need to build *cut.* Stretch out the three sounds: /k/ /ŭ/ /t/. Build *cut* in the pocket chart. Point to each letter and have children blend with you, sound by sound. Then have children blend as you point.

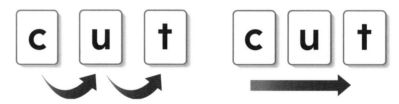

Blending *-ut* Words Replace *c* with *h* and model blending /h/ /ut/, *hut.* Have volunteers blend *-ut* with *b, j,* and *n* to make *but, jut,* and *nut.*

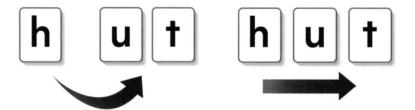

Word Wall Add *cut* to the Word Wall. Children will use *cut* to make rhyming words.

▶ **Apply**

Practice Book page 300 Children complete the page at small group time.

Sunshine State Standards pp. T90–T91   ★ = FCAT Benchmark in Gr. 3–5

★**LA.A.1.1.2.K.2** knows alphabet   ★**LA.A.1.1.3.K.1** identifies high-frequency words
★**LA.A.1.1.2.K.3** knows sounds of alphabet ★**LA.A.1.1.3.K.4** uses sources to build vocabulary
★**LA.A.1.1.2.K.5** basic phonetic principles

Phonics in Action

Reading
Phonics Library

A World of Animals

Reading

Phonics/Decoding Strategy

Teacher-Student Modeling Discuss using the Strategy to read words in the title.

Think Aloud

One word in the title begins with capital C. The sound for C is /k/. I know the sounds for a, n: /ă/ /n/, -an. Let's blend: /k/ /an/, Can. Is Can a real word? Does it make sense in a question? Yes!

Have children read the whole title silently. Ask volunteers to read the title and tell how they blended *It* and *Fit*.

Do a picture walk. Show children the nut on page 14. Ask: **What do squirrels eat?** Write *nut* on the board; model saying the three sounds and then blend /n/ /ut/, *nut*. Ask one child to point and model blending. Ask if the word would make sense in a story about a squirrel family.

▶ Coached Reading

Have children read each page silently before reading with you. Prompts:

pages 10–11 *What are the squirrels doing at the beginning of the story?*

page 11 Have volunteers model how they blended *lug*. Discuss the meaning of *lug*. Then ask: **What two words on this page rhyme? What letters are the same in those words?**

page 15 *What can fit in the house now? Who can model how to blend* nut? *What cannot fit? How can the squirrels solve their problem?*

Phonics Library

Purposes
- apply phonics skills
- apply high-frequency words

It Can Fit
by Thomas Alexander
illustrated by Bernadette Pons

9

See a big van! — 10

He can lug a big jug. It can fit. — 11

She can lug a tan rug. It can fit. — 12

He can lug a hat box. It can fit. — 13

But can a big, fat nut fit? — 14

A big, fat nut can fit. But can not fit. — 15

DAY 3

🏠 **Home Connection**

Children can color the pictures in the take-home version of "It Can Fit." After reading on Day 4, they can take it home to read to family members.

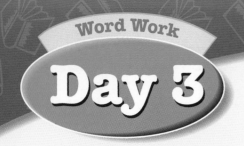

Day 3

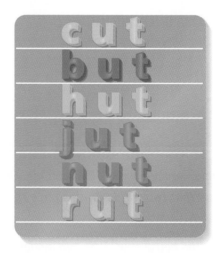

★LA.A.1.1.2.K.5
★LA.A.1.1.3.K.4

Building Words

▶ Word Family: -ut

Using the Letter Cards, model how to build *cut*. *First I'll stretch out the sounds: /k/ /ŭ/ /t/. How many sounds do you hear? The first sound is /k/. I'll put up a c to spell that. The next sound is /ŭ/. What letter spells that? The last sound is /t/. What letter should I choose for that?*

Next, remove the *c* and ask what sounds are left. *Which letter should I add to build* **but?** Model how to read *but* by blending /b/ with /ut/. Continue making and blending *-ut* words by substituting *h, j, n,* and *r.*

Have small groups work together to build *-ut* words. They can use block letters, letter stamps, or other manipulatives in your collection.

Sunshine State Standards pp. T92–T93   ★ = FCAT Benchmark in Gr. 3–5

★**LA.A.1.1.2.K.5** basic phonetic principles   **LA.B.2.1.2.K.1** writes with pictures, words
★**LA.A.1.1.3.K.4** uses sources to build vocabulary   **LA.E.2.1.1.K.2** uses personal interpretations

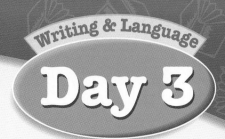

Shared Writing

LA.E.2.1.1.K.2
LA.B.2.1.2.K.1

▶ Writing a Book Report

Viewing and Speaking Tell children they are going to help write a book report about *Feathers for Lunch*. Explain that a *book report* tells what the book is about without giving away the ending.

■ Display the book *Feathers for Lunch*, and page through it with children, inviting them to comment on what happens on each page.

■ Explain that a book report tells about the characters in a book. Ask: **Who are the characters in the book?** (a cat, many birds)

■ Talk about what the characters are doing in the story. **What is the cat trying to do? What are the birds doing? How are the birds warning each other about the cat?**

■ Explain that a book report may be read by people who haven't read a book but might want to read it. Tell children to think about their sentences carefully, so the book report doesn't give away the story ending.

■ Write children's responses on chart paper. Reread their sentences. Explain that their sentences will become part of the book report.

OBJECTIVES

Children

● think of sentences for a book report

MATERIALS

● **Big Book:** *Feathers for Lunch*

DAY 3

This book had a cat.
The cat was hungry.
He tried to catch the birds.
There were many kinds
of birds.

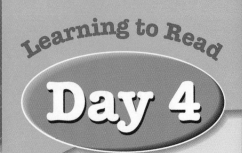

Day 4

Day at a Glance

Learning to Read

Big Book:

Which Pet?

 Phonics:
Reviewing
/b/, /k/, /l/;
Blending
-ut Words,
page T98

Word Work

Building Words, *page T100*

Writing & Language

Interactive Writing, *page T101*

Managing Small Groups

Teacher-Led Group
• Reread **Phonics Library** selection "It Can Fit."
• Begin *Practice Book, 301.*

Independent Groups
• Finish *Practice Book, 301.*
• **Phonics Center:** Theme 10, Week 2, Day 4
• Writing, other Centers

Opening

LA.A.2.1.5.K.2
★LA.A.1.1.2.K.6
★LA.A.1.1.3.K.4

Calendar

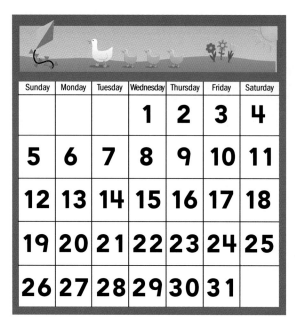

Sunday	Monday	Tuesday	Wednesday	Thursday	Friday	Saturday
			1	2	3	4
5	6	7	8	9	10	11
12	13	14	15	16	17	18
19	20	21	22	23	24	25
26	27	28	29	30	31	

Ask children to compare warm weather to the weather in January. Encourage them to describe how they dressed in each of these seasons.

Daily Message

Interactive Writing Invite the class to blend the word *pet*. Use the word in the message, and ask a volunteer to write it. Have other children contribute letters and words to the message as well.

Annie's pet
puppy likes
bones.

Remind children that the words on the Word Wall are in ABC order. Tell them you will say the alphabet slowly. They should raise their hands when you come to a letter that begins a word on the wall. **A.... are there any words that begin with a? Who will point to them and read them?**

Routines

 ## Daily Phonemic Awareness
Blending and Segmenting Phonemes

Play a guessing game. Display the backs of the Picture Cards for *cut, hut,* and *nut*. Tell children they'll blend sounds to guess the pictures.

- *Let's put some sounds together to name a picture: /c/... /ŭ/... /t/. What do you get?* (cut) Display Picture Card *cut*. Continue with *hut* and *nut*.

- *Now I'll name a picture. You say its sounds like this:* cut ... /c/ /ŭ/ /t/. *Now you try it.* Continue with *hut* and *nut*.

Sunshine State Standards pp. T94–T95
★ = FCAT Benchmark in Gr. 3–5

★**LA.A.1.1.2.K.5** basic phonetic principles
★**LA.A.1.1.2.K.6** print conveys meaning
★**LA.A.1.1.3.K.4** uses sources to build vocabulary
LA.A.2.1.5.K.2 pictures, signs for information
LA.C.1.1.4.K.1 listens for specific information

Phoneme Substitution

- Randomly display Picture Cards for: *cat, can; doll, dot; kit, kiss; pig, pin.* Hold up *cat. What is the last sound in* cat? *If we change the final /t/ to /n/, what word would we have?* Hold up the two pictures and say both words: *cat, can.* Point out that only the last sound is different. Continue with the remaining cards.

Getting Ready to Learn

To help plan their day, tell children that they will

- read the Science Link: *Which Pet?*

- learn to make and read new words in the Phonics Center.

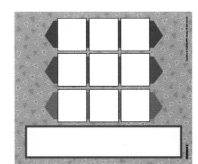

- read a book called "It Can Fit."

It Can Fit
by Thomas Alexander
illustrated by Bernadette Pons

DAY 4

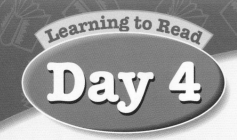

Day 4

Sharing the Big Book
Science Link

OBJECTIVES

Children

- compare and contrast things in a story
- recognize the end of a sentence
- identify end punctuation

Big Book

Which Pet?

Feathers for Lunch

Lois Ehlert

pages 33–39

English Language Learners

LA.E.2.1.1.K.1
★LA.A.1.1.3.K.5

Keep in mind that in many cultures the animals shown may not be kept as pets and that in some cultures animals are not pets at all. Take a picture walk to introduce vocabulary related to the pets and foods shown. Point out that the word *veggies* is a short way of saying *vegetables*.

▶ Building Background

We've read about many types of animals. What do you know about animals that are pets? Name some pets you know. What makes a good pet? Read the title and discuss a few pictures.

Reading for Understanding Pause for discussion as you share the selection.

> **pages 34–37**
>
> ### Strategy: Predict/Infer
>
> **Student Modeling** As you read, ask children to predict which pet likes each kind of food. Ask children to look at the pictures to help them figure it out what foods pets eat. Read on to confirm children's predictions.
>
> ### Comprehension Focus:
> ### Compare and Contrast
>
> **Student Modeling** After reading a few pages, ask: *What has been the same on every page? What does each page show? What is different on each page? Why?*

pages 34–39
Drawing Conclusions

- On each page, have children identify the featured animal and tell what clues they used to figure it out. (Mimi is a hamster; Sam is a dog; Coco is a mouse; Lucky is a bird; Lulu is a cat.) On page 39, have children match the animals and foods. (Kitten eats kitty treats; turtle eats lettuce; macaw eats birdseed.)

pages 34–39
Text Organization: Topic

- *What is this book about?* (what foods different kinds of pets eat)

Sunshine State Standards pp. T96–T97   ★ = FCAT Benchmark in Gr. 3–5

★**LA.A.1.1.2.K.4** concept of words, meaning   **LA.A.1.1.1.K.1** oral predictions
★**LA.A.1.1.3.K.5** develops vocabulary   **LA.A.1.1.4.K.1** strategies to comprehend text
★**LA.A.2.1.1.K.1** main idea from a read-aloud   **LA.B.2.1.2.K.1** writes with pictures, words

Mimi likes veggies!
Which pet is she?
34

Sam likes bones!
Which pet is he?
35

pages 34–35

Coco likes cheese!
Which pet is she?
36

Lucky likes bugs!
Which pet is he?
37

pages 36–37

Lulu likes fish!
Which pet is she?
38

These pets are hungry too!
Which food is best for each one?
39

pages 38–39

pages 34–35

Concepts of Print ★LA.A.1.1.2.K.4

✓ **End of a Sentence/End Punctuation**

■ Point to the exclamation point that ends the first sentence on page 34 and to the question mark that ends the second sentence. Remind children that these marks show where a sentence ends, and tell the reader where to stop. Have children take turns finding the ends of the same kinds of sentences on page 35.

▶ Responding LA.A.1.1.4.K.1

Summarizing Talk about the selection together. Have volunteers summarize the selection, using the photographs as prompts. Ask children to tell which pets they like best and to explain why.

DAY 4

Challenge

LA.B.2.1.2.K.1

Invite children who are ready for a challenge, to create their own books modeled after *Which Pet?* Place a copy of the book in the writing area, along with stapled blank books. Encourage children to copy the question and use their own ideas for different pets.

Sharing the Big Book T97

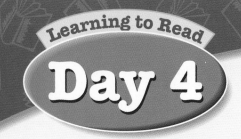
Phonics

 Blending -ut Words

▶ Connect Sounds to Letters

Review Consonants *j, b,* and *c* Ask children to find the *Jj* page of *From Apples to Zebras: A Book of ABC's*. Cover the labels of the pictures and ask children what letter they expect to see first in each word and why. Do the same routine for the *Bb* page and then the *Cc* page.

Reviewing *-ut* Remind children that to build some words they need a vowel ("helper letter"), because every word has at least one of those. Ask which Alphafriend stands for the vowel sound /ŭ/. *(Umbie Umbrella)* Display Umbie and help children think of other words that start with /ŭ/. *(under, upset, us, understand)*

Hold up Letter Cards *c, u,* and *t*. *Watch and listen as I build a word from the Word Wall: /k/ /ŭ/ /t/,* cut, */k/ /ŭ/ /t/,* cut.

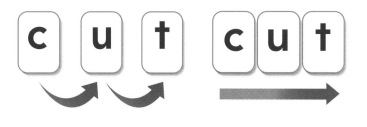

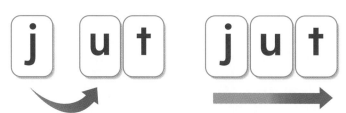

Blending *-ut* Words Remove the Letter Card *c,* and place *j* in front of *-ut*. *Now let's blend my new word: /j/ /ut/,* jut. Continue, having volunteers build and blend *but, hut,* and *nut*. Choose children to use these words in oral sentences.

Sunshine State Standards pp. T98–T99   ★ = FCAT Benchmark in Gr. 3–5

★LA.A.1.1.2.K.2 knows alphabet
★LA.A.1.1.2.K.3 knows sounds of alphabet
★LA.A.1.1.2.K.5 basic phonetic principles

▶ Apply

Build a sentence with the cards shown.

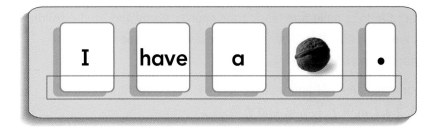

Then replace *nut* with *hut,* and have children read the new sentence: I have a *hut.* Tell children they will build more sentences today in the Phonics Center.

Practice Book page 301 Children will complete this page at small group time.

Phonics Library In groups today, children will also read *-ut* words as they reread the **Phonics Library** story "It Can Fit." See suggestions, page T91.

At Group Time

Phonics Center

★LA.A.1.1.2.K.2, 3, 5

Use the Phonics Center materials for **Theme 10, Week 2, Day 4**.

Practice Book p. 301

Name _____

b → ut _____
c → ut _____
n → ut _____

I like the box _____ not the hat.

Is the _____ for my pet?

"I can _____ it," said Nan.

THEME 10: A World of Animals
Week Two
Phonics: -ut Words

Children
• add letters to -ar to build the words *but, cut,* and *nut*
• write each word to complete the sentences that go with the pictures

Home Connection
Let me read these sentences to you. Then maybe we can draw more pictures to go with the words *but, cut,* and *nut.*

301

DAY 4

Diagnostic Check

If...	➤ You can ...
children have trouble building words,	have them practice making sets of rhyming words with you or a partner.

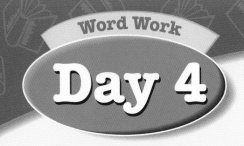

★LA.A.1.1.2.K.5
★LA.A.1.1.3.K.4

Building Words

▶ **Word Families: -ut, -ug, -et**

- Have children say *cut* very slowly and tell you what letters you need to build it in the pocket chart.

- Replace the *c* with known consonants (*b, h, j, r*), building other *-ut* words for children to identify.

- Next, use Letter Cards to build *bug*, saying the sounds slowly and having children tell you what letters to use. Continue building new words by substituting the initial consonants *d, m, j,* and *r*.

- Repeat, this time building *pet* and making new words by substituting initial consonants *b, g, j, l, m, n, p, s, v, w,* and *y*.

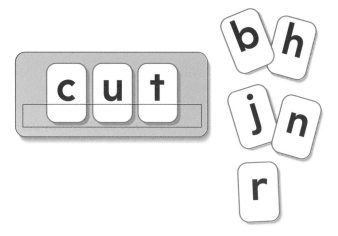

Have groups of children write *-ut, -ug,* and *-et* words on index cards. Have the words used in oral sentences. They can keep a box of words they have learned to build and read.

OBJECTIVES

Children
- build and read *-ut, -ug,* and *-et* words

MATERIALS

- **Letter Cards** *b, c, d, e, g, h, j, l, m, n, p, r, s, t, u, v, w, y*

Sunshine State Standards pp. T100–T101   ★ = FCAT Benchmark in Gr. 3–5

★**LA.A.1.1.2.K.5** basic phonetic principles   **LA.A.2.1.2.K.1** reads for pleasure
★**LA.A.1.1.3.K.1** identifies high-frequency words   **LA.B.2.1.2.K.1** writes with pictures, words
★**LA.A.1.1.3.K.4** uses sources to build vocabulary   **LA.C.1.1.4.K.1** listens for specific information

Interactive Writing

LA.C.1.1.4.K.1
LA.B.2.1.2.K.1
★LA.A.1.1.3.K.1
LA.E.2.1.1.K.1

▶ Writing a Book Report

Listening, Viewing, and Speaking Read the book report from yesterday's Shared Writing activity. Have children add more details. For example, the sentence *There is a cat* could be expanded to *There is a hungry black cat.*

■ Invite children to expand on other sentences in a similar manner. Remind them of what they know about exact naming words, describing words, and action words.

■ Let children page through *Feathers for Lunch* for details to add. As you rewrite the sentences, invite children to write high-frequency words, and the last two letters of words that rhyme with *an, at, it, dig, pot, box, wet, hen, bug,* and *cut.*

■ Ask children to think of a title that will make their friends want to read the report.

■ Invite individuals to give their evaluations of the book. Add these to the bottom of the report, preceded by the name of the child who contributed the comment. Let children write their own names and other letters and words they know.

■ Display the report where children can try reading it alone or with partners.

At Group Time

Writing Center

LA.A.2.1.2.K.1
LA.B.2.1.2.K.1

Fill the Writing Center with familiar books about animals. Invite children to make their own book reports about books they choose themselves. Children can draw several pictures showing the most important events in the book. Remind children to show what the characters are doing but to keep the ending a surprise!

A wolf is at the door.

Portfolio Opportunity

After displaying the finished product from a group writing activity, you might want to save it for conference time. Write contributors' names in small print next to the sentences they offered for the work.

DAY 4

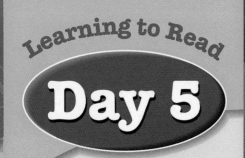

Day at a Glance

Learning to Read

Revisiting the Literature:

The Tale of the Three Little Pigs, Feathers for Lunch, Which Pet?, "It Can Fit"

☑ **Phonics: Initial Consonants b, c, l; -ut, -ug, -en Words;** *page T106*

Word Work

Building Words, *page T108*

Writing & Language

Independent Writing, *page T109*

Managing Small Groups

Teacher-Led Group
- Reread familiar **Phonics Library** selections.
- Begin *Practice Book, 302,* **Blackline Master 36.**

Independent Groups
- Reread **Phonics Library** selections.
- Finish *Practice Book, 302,* **Blackline Master 36.**
- Centers

Opening

LA.A.2.1.5.K.2
★LA.A.1.1.2.K.6
★LA.A.1.1.3.K.4

Calendar

Sunday	Monday	Tuesday	Wednesday	Thursday	Friday	Saturday
			1	2	3	4
5	6	7	8	9	10	11
12	13	14	15	16	17	18
19	20	21	22	23	24	25
26	27	28	29	30	31	

See if children can name the day, month, date, and year without help from you. Then start the sentence *A day in this month can be _____,* and ask children to think of describing words to complete it.

Daily Message

Modeled Writing Put a useful saying in today's message, and talk about its meaning. How does it remind people about something important?

The early bird gets the worm.

Read the Word Wall together. Then play a rhyming game: *I'm going to find a word on the wall that rhymes with* nut ... Cut *rhymes with* nut. *Now raise your hand when you hear a word that rhymes with* day.

Routines

✓ Daily Phonemic Awareness
Blending and Segmenting Phonemes

- Display "Giraffes" on page 42 of *Higglety Pigglety.*

- Read the poem, stopping before *huff.* *I'll say the sounds, and you guess the word: /h/ /ŭ/ /f/. Say the sounds with me: /h/ /ŭ/ /f/. What word is it?* (huff) *Who will show us what* huff *means?*

- Continue, segmenting *hoot* and *keep.* Have children blend them.

- Now reverse the procedure. Say each whole word *(huff, hoot, keep)* slowly, and have children say its separate sounds.

✓ Phoneme Substitution

- Next, help children replace the final phoneme to make new words. *What if I changed /f/ at the end of huff to /g/: /h/ /ŭ/ /f/ changes to /h/ /ŭ/ /g/. What is the word?* (hug)

Giraffes
Don't
Huff

Giraffes don't huff or hoot or howl
They never grump, they never growl
They never roar, they never riot,
They eat green leaves
And just keep quiet.

by Karla Kuskin

Higglety Pigglety: A Book of Rhymes, page 42

Getting Ready to Learn

To help plan their day, tell children that they will

- reread and talk about all the books they've read this week.

- take home a story they can read.

- draw and write a report about a favorite book in their journals.

Sunshine State Standards pp. T102–T103
★ = FCAT Benchmark in Gr. 3–5

★LA.A.1.1.2.K.5 basic phonetic principles
★LA.A.1.1.2.K.6 print conveys meaning
★LA.A.1.1.3.K.4 uses sources to build vocabulary
LA.A.2.1.5.K.2 pictures, signs for information
LA.C.1.1.4.K.1 listens for specific information

It Can Fit
by Thomas Alexander
illustrated by Bernadette Pons

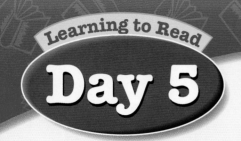

★LA.A.2.1.1.K.1
LA.C.3.1.2.K.1
★LA.A.1.1.2.K.5
LA.A.1.1.4.K.1
FCAT Benchmark in Gr. 3–5

Revisiting the Literature

▶ Literature Discussion

Invite children to compare all the selections you shared this week. First, use these suggestions to recall the selections:

■ Have volunteers tell about the different houses in *the Tale of the Three Little Pigs.*

■ Page through *Feathers for Lunch* with children, reading the bird calls. Talk about why the calls were important in the story and how the birds stayed safe from the cat.

■ Have children choose their favorite animals in *Which Pet?* and tell why.

■ Reread "It Can Fit" together. Choose children to model blending *But* and *nut.*

Ask children to vote on their favorite book this week. Read the winning book aloud.

Comprehension Focus: Compare and Contrast

Comparing Books Remind children that thinking about how things are alike and different helps readers make sense of what they read. Browse through each selection with children, inviting them to name things that were the same and things that were different in the stories. Ask questions such as: *What was the wolf trying to do in* The Tale of the Three Little Pigs? *How was he like the cat in* Feathers for Lunch?

Technology

LA.B.2.1.3.K.1

www.eduplace.com

Log on to **Education Place** for more activities relating to *A World of Animals.*

www.bookadventure.org

This Internet reading-incentive program provides thousands of titles for children to read.

Sunshine State Standards pp. T104–T105   ★ = FCAT Benchmark in Gr. 3–5

★**LA.A.1.1.2.K.3** knows sounds of alphabet   **LA.A.1.1.4.K.1** strategies to comprehend text
★**LA.A.1.1.2.K.5** basic phonetic principles   **LA.A.2.1.2.K.1** reads for pleasure
★**LA.A.2.1.1.K.1** main idea from a read-aloud   **LA.B.2.1.3.K.1** uses computer for writing

LA.A.1.1.4.K.1
LA.C.3.1.1.K.1
★LA.A.1.1.2.K.3, 5
LA.A.2.1.2.K.1

Building Fluency

▶ Rereading Familiar Texts

Phonics Library: "It Can Fit" Remind children that they've learned the new word *he* this week and that they've learned to read words with *-ut*. As children reread the **Phonics Library** story "It Can Fit" have them look for words with *-ut*.

Review Feature several **Phonics Library** titles in the Book Corner. Have children demonstrate their growing skills by choosing one to reread aloud, alternating pages with a partner. From time to time, ask children to point out words or pages that they can read more easily now.

Oral Reading Sometimes a child misreads a word so that the sentence does not make sense. If you hear "It can foot" instead of "It can fit," for example, repeat the sentence as the child said it and ask if it makes sense in the story. Remind the child to think about the meaning of the sentence, and then go back and analyze the letters/sounds again.

It Can Fit
by Thomas Alexander
illustrated by Bernadette Pons

Ken and Jen
by Thomas Alexander
illustrated by Thierry Courtin

Ben
by Ann Spivey
illustrated by Susan Calitri

Blackline Master 36 Children complete the page and take it home to share their reading progress.

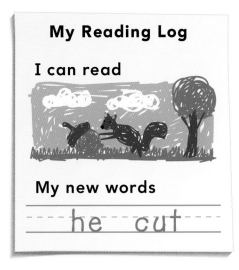

My Reading Log

I can read

My new words

he cut

DAY 5

Home Connection

Remind children to share the **take-home version** of "It Can Fit" with their families.

Revisiting the Literature/ Building Fluency

(T105)

Day 5

★LA.A.1.1.2.K.5

 **Phonics Review**

 Consonants, Word Families

OBJECTIVES

Children

- make and read words with initial consonants and short *u* + *g*, short *u* + *t*, short *e* + *n*
- make sentences with high-frequency words.

MATERIALS

- **Word Cards** *a, and, are, for, go, have, he, here, I, is, like, my, play, said, see, she, the, to*
- **Picture Cards** *dog, fish, toast,* and others you choose
- **Punctuation Cards:** period, question mark

▶ Review

Tell children that they will take turns being word builders and word readers today. Have a group of word builders stand with you at the chalkboard.

- *Let me see you write* bug. *First, count the sounds, and then write a letter for each sound.* Check children's work.

- *Now erase* b *and write* r *in its place. Read the new word to yourself. Then call on one of the word readers to say it.*

- A new group changes places with the first one. At your direction they erase the *r*, write *d*, and ask word readers to say the new word.

- Continue, giving everyone a turn to build words by replacing letters. Examples: *mug, lug, hug; hut, jut, nut, rut, cut.* Begin again with *den, hen, Ben, men, pen, ten.*

- Children can also write the words at their work stations and check their work with chalkboard examples. Monitor individuals' work to ensure that children's responses are correct.

Sunshine State Standards pp. T106–T107   ★ = FCAT Benchmark in Gr. 3–5

★**LA.A.1.1.2.K.5** basic phonetic principles
★**LA.A.1.1.3.K.1** identifies high-frequency words

High-Frequency Word Review

 I, see, my, like, a, to, and, go, is, here, for, have, said, are, he, play, she, the

▶ Review

Prepare cards for *cut* and *cat*. Then give each small group the Word Cards, Picture Cards, and a Punctuation Card needed to make a sentence. Each child holds one card. Children stand and arrange themselves to make a sentence for others to read.

▶ Apply

Practice Book page 302 Children can complete this page independently and read it to you during small group time.

Phonics Library Have children take turns reading aloud to the class. Each child might read one page of "It Can Fit" or a favorite **Phonics Library** selection from the previous theme. Remind readers to share the pictures!

Discussion questions:

■ *Do you hear any rhyming words in either story? What letters are the same in those words?*

■ *Find a word that starts with the same sound as* Callie Cat's *name. What is the letter? What is the sound?* Repeat for for *Benny Bear* and *Larry Lion.*

■ *This week we added the word* he *to the Word Wall. Look through "It Can Fit" for that word.*

Practice Book p. 302

Portfolio Opportunity

Save the **Practice Book** page to show children's mastery of high-frequency words.

Diagnostic Check

If . . .	You can . . .
children pause at high-frequency words in **Phonics Library** selections,	have children practice finding these words on the Word Wall with a partner.

DAY 5

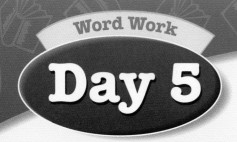

Day 5

★LA.A.1.1.2.K.5
★LA.A.1.1.3.K.4

Building Words

▶ Word Families

Choose a child to tell you what letters you need to build *cut*. Along the bottom of the pocket chart, line up the letters *b, h, j, n,* and *r*. **Who can tell me how to change** cut **to** hut**? Which letter should I take away? What should I add?** Now ask volunteers to replace letters to build words you say. For each completed word, have the child point to the letters while the class blends the sounds. On chart paper, list all the word families you make, and reread the list together.

Suggested words: *but, jut, nut, rut; bug, jug, dug, mug, rug; wet, set, met, let, vet, pet, yet.*

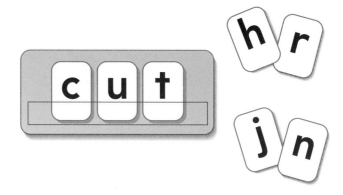

Have small groups work together to build *-ut* words on white boards or with manipulative letters. They can add new words to the Word Bank section of their journals and add appropriate pictures. Add any new words to posted lists of word families. Encourage children to build sentences using the pattern words and the high-frequency words on the Word Wall.

OBJECTIVES

Children

- build and read *-ut, -ug,* and *-et* words

MATERIALS

- **Letter Cards:** *b, c, d, e, g, h, j, l, m, n, p, r, s, t, u, v, w, y*

Sunshine State Standards pp. T108–T109   ★ = FCAT Benchmark in Gr. 3–5

★**LA.A.1.1.2.K.5** basic phonetic principles   **LA.B.2.1.2.K.1** writes with pictures, words
★**LA.A.1.1.3.K.4** uses sources to build vocabulary   **LA.E.2.1.1.K.2** uses personal interpretations

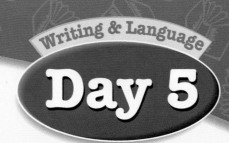
Independent Writing

LA.B.2.1.2.K.1
LA.E.2.1.1.K.2

Journals Together, reread the charts from this week's shared and interactive writing. Point out all the bird names and rhyming words that were used.

- Pass out the journals.

- Display the literature children read this week. *What are your favorite animal books? Are any of them told in rhymes? Which one would you like to write a report about in your journal? What did you like best about the book? You could draw a picture of that or write about it in your report.*

- On chart paper, write *I like* _____. Children can complete the sentence with the name of the selection they choose and draw or write about why they like it. Remind children that they can use the animal words posted in the room as they write.

- Invite children to share what they've written.

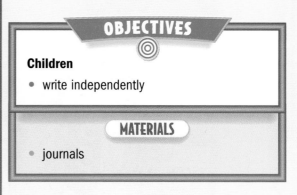

OBJECTIVES

Children
- write independently

MATERIALS
- journals

Teacher's Note

An alphabet chart and a list of favorite words from the theme can help prompt hesitant writers to write independently.

Literature for Week 3
Different texts for different purposes

Teacher Read Alouds:
- **Run Away!**
- **The Tale of the Three Little Pigs**
- **Henny Penny**

Purposes

- oral language
- listening strategy
- comprehension skill

Big Books:

Higglety Pigglety: A Book of Rhymes

Purposes

- oral language development
- phonemic awareness

From Apples to Zebras: A Book of ABC's

Purposes

- alphabet recognition
- letters and sounds

Big Books: Main Selections

Purposes

- concepts of print
- reading strategy
- story language
- comprehension skills

Also available in Little Big Book and audiotape

Also available in Little Big Book and audiotape

Leveled Books

Baby Animals Play

Science Link

Which Pet?

Science Link

Also in the Big Books:
- Science Links

Purposes

- reading strategies
- comprehension skills
- concepts of print

Phonics Library

Phonics Library

A World of Animals

Also available in Take-Home version

Purposes

- applying phonics skills and high-frequency words

On My Way Practice Reader

Animals at Play
by Wil Perry

Animals at Play

by Wil Perry
page T155

Houghton Mifflin

Little Readers for Guided Reading
Collection K

Houghton Mifflin Classroom Bookshelf
Level K

Technology

www.eduplace.com

Log on to *Education Place* for more activities relating to *A World of Animals*.

www.bookadventure.org

This free Internet reading-incentive program provides thousands of titles for students to read.

Suggested Daily Routines

Instructional Goals

Learning to Read

✓ **Phonemic Awareness:** Blending and Segmenting Phonemes, Phoneme Substitution

Strategy Focus: Question, Summarize

✓ **Comprehension Skill:** Story Structure: Plot

✓ **Phonics Skills**

Phonemic Awareness: Beginning Sounds /d/, /j/, /n/, /w/

Initial Consonants *D, d, J, j, N, n, W, w*

Compare and Review: Initial Consonants: *d, j, n, w*

✓ **High-Frequency Review Words:** *are, he*

✓ **Concepts of Print:** Beginning and End of a Sentence; End Punctuation

Word Work

High-Frequency Word Practice:
Word Families: *-ug, -ut, -en*

Writing & Language

Vocabulary Skill: Using Order Words, Animal Names

Writing Skills: Writing Directions

Sunshine State Standards Achieved Each Day

LA.A = Reading
LA.B = Writing
LA.C = Listening/Viewing/Speaking
LA.D = Language
LA.E = Literature

★ = FCAT Benchmark in Grades 3–5

Day 1

Opening Routines, *T116–T117*   LA.A.2.1.5.K.2
                                          ★LA.A.1.1.2.K.5, 6
Word Wall   ★LA.A.1.1.3.K.4

- **Phonemic Awareness:** Blending and Segmenting Phonemes, Phoneme Substitution ★LA.A.1.1.2.K.2, 3, 5

Teacher Read Aloud
Henny Penny, T118–T121   LA.C.1.1.1.K.2
- **Strategy:** Summarize   LA.A.1.1.4.K.1
- **Comprehension:** Story Structure: Plot
                                   ★LA.E.1.1.2.K.1

Phonics
Instruction
- Phonemic Awareness, Beginning Sound /d/, /j/, /n/, /w/, *T122–T123;* ★LA.A.1.1.2.K.2, 3, 5
- *Practice Book, 305–306*

High-Frequency Word Practice
- Words: *and, can, he, here, play, said, I, she,* T124   ★LA.A.1.1.3.K.1

Oral Language
- Using Order Words, *T125*   ★LA.E.1.1.2.K.1

Day 2

Opening Routines, *T126–T127*   LA.A.2.1.5.K.2
                                          ★LA.A.1.1.2.K.5, 6
Word Wall   ★LA.A.1.1.3.K.4

- **Phonemic Awareness:** Blending and Segmenting Phonemes, Phoneme Substitution

Sharing the Big Book
Splash!, T128–T129   LA.C.1.1.1.K.2
- **Strategy:** Summarize   LA.A.1.1.4.K.1
- **Comprehension:** Story Structure: Plot
                                   ★LA.E.1.1.2.K.1

Phonics
Instruction, Practice
- Initial Consonants *d, j, n,* and *w, T130–T131*
                                   ★LA.A.1.1.2.K.2, 3, 5
- *Practice Book, 307*

High-Frequency Words
- Review Words: *are, he, T132–T133*
                                   ★LA.A.1.1.3.K.1
- *Practice Book, 308*

High-Frequency Word Practice
- Words: *A, a, is, The, the,* T134   ★LA.A.1.1.3.K.1

Vocabulary Expansion
- Animal Names, *T135*   ★LA.A.1.1.3.K.3, 4
- Viewing, *T135*   LA.C.2.1.1.K.1

★ **LA.A.1.1.2.K.2** knows alphabet
★ **LA.A.1.1.2.K.3** knows sounds of alphabet
★ **LA.A.1.1.2.K.5** basic phonetic principles
★ **LA.A.1.1.2.K.6** print conveys meaning
★ **LA.A.1.1.3.K.1** identifies high frequency words
★ **LA.A.1.1.3.K.4** uses sources to build vocabulary
★ **LA.E.1.1.2.K.1** sequence of events, setting
  LA.A.1.1.4.K.1 strategies to comprehend text
  LA.A.2.1.5.K.2 pictures, signs for information
  LA.C.1.1.1.K.2 listens to oral language

★ **LA.A.1.1.2.K.2** knows alphabet
★ **LA.A.1.1.2.K.3** knows sounds of alphabet
★ **LA.A.1.1.2.K.5** basic phonetic principles
★ **LA.A.1.1.2.K.6** print conveys meaning
★ **LA.A.1.1.3.K.1** identifies high frequency words
★ **LA.A.1.1.3.K.3** sorts words from categories
★ **LA.A.1.1.3.K.4** uses sources to build vocabulary
★ **LA.E.1.1.2.K.1** sequence of events, setting
  LA.A.1.1.4.K.1 strategies to comprehend text
  LA.A.2.1.5.K.2 pictures, signs for information
  LA.C.1.1.1.K.2 listens to oral language
  LA.C.2.1.1.K.1 main idea in nonprint

 Leveled Books, p. T155   LA.A.2.1.2.K.1

Half-Day Kindergarten
Focus on lessons for tested skills. ✔
Then choose other activities as time allows.

 *Technology*
Florida Lesson Planner CD-ROM
Customize your planning for *the week* with the Florida Lesson Planner.

 Key correlations are provided in this chart. Additional correlations are provided at point of use.

Day 3

Opening Routines, *T136–T137*   LA.A.2.1.5.K.2
★LA.A.1.1.2.K.5, 6
★LA.A.1.1.3.K.4

Word Wall

- **Phonemic Awareness:** Blending and Segmenting Phonemes, Phoneme Substitution   ★LA.A.1.1.2.K.2, 3, 5

Sharing the Big Book
Feathers for Lunch, T138–T139   LA.C.1.1.1.K.2
- **Strategy:** Summarize   LA.A.1.1.4.K.1
- **Comprehension:** Story Structure: Plot, *T138; Practice Book, 309*   ★LA.E.1.1.2.K.1
- **Concepts of Print:** Beginning and End of a Sentence, *T139*   ★LA.A.1.1.2.K.1, 4

Phonics

Practice, Application
- Consonant *b, T140–T141*   ★LA.A.1.1.2.K.2, 3, 5

Instruction
- Blending *-ug* and *-ut* Words *T140–T141; Practice Book, 310*   ★LA.A.1.1.2.K.5
- **Phonics Library:** "The Bug Hut," *T141*   ★LA.A.1.1.2.K.3, 5
★LA.A.1.1.3.K.1

Building Words
- Word Families: *-ug, -ut, T142*   ★LA.A.1.1.2.K.5
★LA.A.1.1.3.K.4

✎ **Shared Writing**
- Writing Directions, *T143*   LA.B.1.1.2.K.1
- Listening, Speaking, and Viewing, *T143*
LA.C.1.1.1.K.1

Day 4

Opening Routines, *T144–T145*   LA.A.2.1.5.K.2
★LA.A.1.1.2.K.5, 6
★LA.A.1.1.3.K.4

Word Wall

- **Phonemic Awareness:** Blending and Segmenting Phonemes, Phoneme Substitution   ★LA.A.1.1.2.K.2, 3, 5

Sharing the Big Book
Science Links: "Baby Animals Play," "Which Pet?," *T146–T147*   ★LA.A.2.1.1.K.1
- **Strategy:** Question   LA.A.1.1.4.K.1
- **Comprehension:** Story Structure: Plot
- **Concepts of Print:** Beginning and End of a Sentence   ★LA.A.1.1.2.K.1

Phonics

Practice
- Blending *-ug* and *-ut* Words, *T148–T149; Practice Book, 311*   ★LA.A.1.1.2.K.2, 3, 5

Building Words
- Word Families: *-ug, -ut, -en, T150*   ★LA.A.1.1.2.K.5
★LA.A.1.1.3.K.4

✎ **Interactive Writing**
- Writing Directions, *T151*   LA.B.1.1.2.K.1, 3
- Viewing and Speaking, *T151*   LA.C.2.1.1.K.1
LA.C.3.1.3.K.1

Day 5

Opening Routines, *T152–T153*   LA.A.2.1.5.K.2
★LA.A.1.1.2.K.5, 6
★LA.A.1.1.3.K.4

Word Wall

- **Phonemic Awareness:** Blending and Segmenting Phonemes, Phoneme Substitution

Revisiting the Literature
Comprehension: Story Structure: Plot, *T154*   ★LA.E.1.1.2.K.1
Building Fluency
- **On My Way Practice Reader:** "Animals at Play," *T155*   LA.A.1.1.1.K.1   LA.A.1.1.4.K.1
LA.A.2.1.2.K.1   LA.E.2.1.1.K.1

Phonics Review
- Consonants, Word Families, *T156*   ★LA.A.1.1.2.K.5
★LA.A.1.1.3.K.4

High-Frequency Word Review
- Words, *I, see, my, like, a, to, and, go, is, here, for, have, said, play, she, are, he, T157; Practice Book, 312*   ★LA.A.1.1.3.K.1

Building Words
- Word Families: *-ug, -ut, -en, -et, -ot, T158*   ★LA.A.1.1.2.K.5
★LA.A.1.1.3.K.4

✎ **Interactive Writing**
- Journals: Directions, *T159*   LA.B.2.1.1.K.1

★ **LA.A.1.1.2.K.1** how print is organized
★ **LA.A.1.1.2.K.2** knows alphabet
★ **LA.A.1.1.2.K.3** knows sounds of alphabet
★ **LA.A.1.1.2.K.4** concept of words, meaning
★ **LA.A.1.1.2.K.5** basic phonetic principles
★ **LA.A.1.1.2.K.6** print conveys meaning
★ **LA.A.1.1.3.K.1** identifies high frequency words
★ **LA.A.1.1.3.K.4** uses sources to build vocabulary
★ **LA.E.1.1.2.K.1** sequence of events, setting
LA.A.1.1.4.K.1 strategies to comprehend text
LA.A.2.1.5.K.2 pictures, signs for information
LA.B.1.1.2.K.1 dictates messages
LA.C.1.1.1.K.1 follows 2-step oral directions
LA.C.1.1.1.K.2 listens to oral language

★ **LA.A.1.1.2.K.1** how print is organized
★ **LA.A.1.1.2.K.2** knows alphabet
★ **LA.A.1.1.2.K.3** knows sounds of alphabet
★ **LA.A.1.1.2.K.5** basic phonetic principles
★ **LA.A.1.1.2.K.6** print conveys meaning
★ **LA.A.1.1.3.K.4** uses sources to build vocabulary
★ **LA.A.2.1.1.K.1** main idea from a read-aloud
LA.A.1.1.4.K.1 strategies to comprehend text
LA.A.2.1.5.K.2 pictures, signs for information
LA.B.1.1.2.K.1 dictates messages
LA.B.1.1.2.K.3 able to sequence events
LA.C.2.1.1.K.1 main idea in nonprint
LA.C.3.1.3.K.1 uses speaking vocabulary

★ **LA.A.1.1.2.K.5** basic phonetic principles
★ **LA.A.1.1.2.K.6** print conveys meaning
★ **LA.A.1.1.3.K.1** identifies high frequency words
★ **LA.A.1.1.3.K.4** uses sources to build vocabulary
★ **LA.E.1.1.2.K.1** sequence of events, setting
LA.A.1.1.1.K.1 oral predictions
LA.A.1.1.4.K.1 strategies to comprehend text
LA.A.2.1.2.K.1 reads for pleasure
LA.A.2.1.5.K.2 pictures, signs for information
LA.B.2.1.1.K.1 uses pictures, words
LA.E.2.1.1.K.1 relates own life to a read-aloud

✎ **Independent Writing Activity, p. T159**   LA.B.2.1.1.K.1

Week 3

Setting up the Centers

Teacher's Note

Management Tip Use a video camera to record children's activities in the Centers this week. Show different children in each Center, and invite them to explain each activity and tell why they like it. Next year, show the tape to your new kindergarten class to pique their interest about the exciting things they will learn in school.

*LA.A.1.1.2.K.2, 3, 5

Phonics Center

Materials • Phonics Center materials for Theme 10, Week 3

Children review the sounds for *d, w,* and *n,* and they make words with the letters *b, h,* and the word families *-ug* and *-ut.* They also build sentences with Word Cards. See pages T123, T131, and T149 for this week's Phonics Center activities.

LA.A.2.1.2.K.1

Book Center

Materials • books about animals

Add more books about animals to the Center for children to compare: nonfiction books with photographs, storybooks with illustrations, and books with several habitats. See page T129 for this week's Book Center suggestion.

Bugs *from the World Wildlife Fund*
Do Pigs Have Stripes? *by Melanie Walsh*
Northwest Animal Babies *by Art Wolfe and Andrea Helman*
The Very Hungry Caterpillar *by Eric Carle*

Sunshine State Standards pp. T58–T59   ★ = FCAT Benchmark in Gr. 3–5

THEME 10: **A World of Animals**

T114

★LA.A.1.1.2.K.2 knows alphabet   ★LA.A.1.1.2.K.5 basic phonetic principles
★LA.A.1.1.2.K.3 knows sounds of alphabet   LA.A.2.1.2.K.1 reads for pleasure

LA.B.1.1.2.K.3

Writing Center

Materials • large sheets of paper • lined and unlined paper • crayons or markers

Children put scenes in order for a four-page book, create a new page for *Baby Animals Play*, and make a class book of directions for pet care. See pages T125 and T151 for this week's Writing Center activities.

MA.C.1.1.1

➕➗ Math Center

Materials • art paper • crayons or markers • glue • craft sticks • feathers

Children create shape puppets from paper cut into ovals, circles, and triangles. They make bird or cat puppets and use them to act out the story *Feathers for Lunch*. See page T139 for the Math Center activity.

SC.D.1.1.3

Science Center

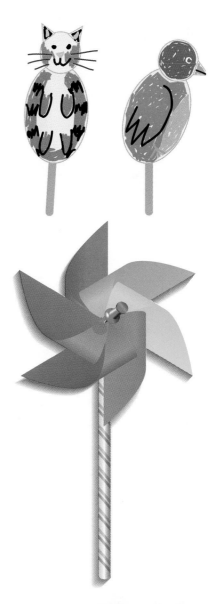

Materials • paper squares • straws • paper fasteners • turkey basters • paper fans

Children make pinwheels and observe how they are affected by wind from different sources. See page T119 for this week's Science Center activity.

LA.B.1.1.2.K.3 able to sequence events
MA.C.1.1.1 understands 2-D, 3-D shapes

SC.D.1.1.5 recognizes patterns in weather

Day 1

Day at a Glance

Learning to Read

Teacher Read Aloud:

Henny Penny

✓ Reviewing
/d/, /j/,
/n/,/w/,
page T122

Word Work

✓ **High-Frequency Word Practice,**
page T124

Writing & Language

Oral Language, *page T125*

Managing Small Groups
Teacher-Led Group
• Begin *Practice Book, 303–306.*
• Reread familiar **Phonics Library** selections.

Independent Groups
• Finish *Practice Book, 303–306.*
• **Phonics Center:** Theme 10, Week 3, Day 1
• Writing, Science, other Centers

Opening

LA.A.2.1.5.K.2
★LA.A.1.1.2.K.6
★LA.A.1.1.3.K.4

Calendar

Sunday	Monday	Tuesday	Wednesday	Thursday	Friday	Saturday
			1	2	3	4
5	6	7	8	9	10	11
12	13	14	15	16	17	18
19	20	21	22	23	24	25
26	27	28	29	30	31	

Lead children in a chant of the days of the week. Then point to the days in random order, say the beginning sound, and have children say the word: /s/... (Sunday) /m/... (Monday).

Daily Message

Interactive Writing In today's message, ask the question shown and explain that the answer is on the Word Wall. Ask the first child who comes up with the correct answer to write it in the message. Continue with more questions.

What animal lives on a farm and lays eggs?
hen
We will read a story about this animal today.

Have children chant the spelling of each word on the wall today. Children can tap with rhythm sticks, tapping one beat for each letter: **T-h-e** *spells* the *and* **h-e** *spells* he *and* **a-r-e** *spells* are.

Routines

 Daily Phonemic Awareness
Blending and Segmenting Phonemes

Read "Notice" on page 20 of *Higglety Pigglety*. Play a "break-apart" game. *I will break apart a word from the poem. Listen to the sounds. See if you can put them back together to make a word:/ d / / ǒ / / g /. Say the sounds with me:/ d / / ǒ / / g /. What is the word?* (dog) Continue, segmenting the words *cat, hat,* and *got.*

Now reverse the procedure. Say some other two- or three-sound words, and have children say the separate sounds to partners.

Notice

I have a dog,
I had a cat.
I've got a frog
Inside my hat.

by David McCord

20

Phoneme Substitution

Make some silly rhymes to help children manipulate sounds. Tell them to listen as you recite "Notice," making all the animal names start with / b /: *bog, bat, brog.* Invite children to chant the silly version with you. Then have them try it with / p / (pog, pat, prog) and / t / (tog, tat, trog).

Higglety Pigglety: A Book of Rhymes, page 20

Getting Ready to Learn

To help plan their day, tell children that they will

Sunshine State Standards pp. T116–T117
★ = FCAT Benchmark in Gr. 3–5

★LA.A.1.1.2.K.5 basic phonetic principles
★LA.A.1.1.2.K.6 print conveys meaning
★LA.A.1.1.3.K.4 uses sources to build vocabulary
LA.A.2.1.5.K.2 pictures, signs for information
LA.C.1.1.4.K.1 listens for specific information

- listen to a story called *Henny Penny.*

- revisit some familiar Alphafriends.

- experiment with pinwheels and moving air in the Science Center.

 ★LA.A.1.1.2.K.5
LA.C.1.1.4.K.1

DAY 1

 Opening Routines T117

Read Aloud

Purposes • oral language • listening strategy • comprehension skill

---

Selection Summary
In this folktale, the wind drops something on Henny Penny's head, and she jumps to the conclusion that the sky is falling. On her way to tell the king, she and her friends are enticed to Fox's house for "dinner." Realizing that *they* are the dinner, Henny Penny and company escape just in time.

Key Concepts
Jumping to conclusions

MEETING INDIVIDUAL NEEDS

English Language Learners

★LA.A.1.1.3.K.4
Preteach the following key vocabulary: *sky falling, tell, stop, gobble, dinner.* Make sure the children understand the significance of the fox and how the fox would want to eat the birds.

LA.C.1.1.1.K.2   LA.A.1.1.4.K.1
LA.A.1.1.1.K.1   ★LA.E.1.1.2.K.1
LA.C.1.1.1.K.2

Teacher Read Aloud
Oral Language/Comprehension

▶ **Building Background**

Talk about what happens on a windy day. *Have you ever seen things fly around in the wind or drop from trees?*

Also talk about the meaning of the saying "jumping to conclusions." To show that everyone makes mistakes, you might share a funny anecdote about a wrong conclusion of your own. *Have you ever done something without thinking it through? What happened?*

Strategy: Summarize

Introduce *Henny Penny,* sharing the illustration on T121.

Teacher Modeling Tell children that as they listen, they should think about the important ideas and how they fit together.

Think Aloud

The picture shows me a lot of animals, all following a hen. I think the important ideas will be where the hen is leading the others and why. Let's listen for that as we read.

✓ **Comprehension Focus:**
Story Structure: Plot

Teacher Modeling Remind children that among the important events in a story are usually the problem and the solution.

Think Aloud

We usually learn about the problem at the beginning of a story. The middle of the story tells about the things the characters do to try to solve their problem. At the end we find out what worked. Let's look for the problem and what the characters do to solve it. Knowing this will help us retell the most important events, too!

Sunshine State Standards pp. T118–T119   ★ = FCAT Benchmark in Gr. 3–5

★**LA.A.1.1.3.K.4** uses sources to build vocabulary   **LA.A.1.1.4.K.1** strategies to comprehend text
★**LA.E.1.1.2.K.1** sequence of events, setting   **LA.C.1.1.1.K.2** listens to oral language
LA.A.1.1.1.K.1 oral predictions   **SC.D.1.1.3** recognizes patterns in weather

▶ Listening to the Story

Read the story aloud, stopping for the questions noted within the text. As the list of characters grows, hesitate before each name to help children predict and chime in. Start a circle map and fill it in as characters are introduced. Note that the Read Aloud art is also available on the back of the Theme Poster.

▶ Responding

Summarizing the Story Help children summarize the important parts:

■ *What happened in the beginning that made Henny Penny run?*

■ *Whom did Henny Penny meet on the way? How did the fox trick the birds?*

■ *How did Henny Penny and her friends escape from the fox?*

Add **Blackline Master 153** pictures to the circle map so children can use it to retell the story.

Practice Book pages 303–304 Children will complete the pages at small group time.

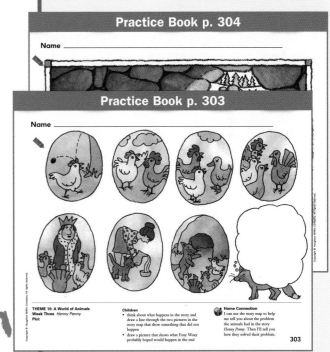

Practice Book p. 304

Practice Book p. 303

SC.D.1.1.3

At Group Time

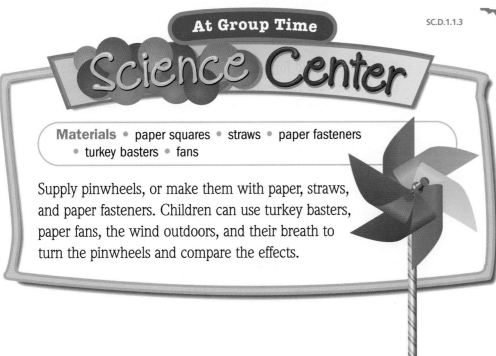

Science Center

Materials • paper squares • straws • paper fasteners • turkey basters • fans

Supply pinwheels, or make them with paper, straws, and paper fasteners. Children can use turkey basters, paper fans, the wind outdoors, and their breath to turn the pinwheels and compare the effects.

Teacher's Note

Make a circle map with the story character names listed clockwise on the circumference of a circle. Children can use the map to retell the story.

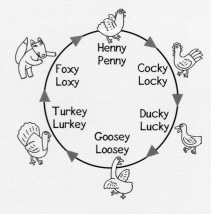

Day 1

Henny Penny

An Old English Folktale

It was a very windy day. *Whooooo! Whooooo!* went the wind. Nuts, berries, leaves, and twigs were scattered on the ground all around.

Henny Penny was searching for something tasty to eat, when all of a sudden, *plunk!* Something landed on her head.

"Oh me, oh my!" said Henny Penny. "The sky is falling. I must go and tell the king." So she hurried off.

As Henny Penny went along, she met Cocky Locky. "Where are you going, Henny Penny?" he asked.

"The sky is falling. I must go and tell the king," said Henny Penny.

"Oh my! Oh my! Let me come with you," said Cocky Locky.

"Of course!" said Henny Penny. "But we must hurry!" (**Ask:** *Why do you think Henny Penny is in such a hurry? What is her problem?*)

As Henny Penny and Cocky Locky hurried along together, they met Ducky Lucky. "Where are you going?" she asked.

"The sky is falling. We must go and tell the king," said Henny Penny.

"Oh my! Oh my! Let me come with you," said Ducky Lucky.

"Of course!" said Henny Penny. "But we must hurry."

As Henny Penny, Cocky Locky, and Ducky Lucky hurried along together, they met Goosey Loosey. "Where are you going?" she asked.

"The sky is falling. We must go and tell the king," said Henny Penny.

"Oh my! Oh my! Let me come with you," said Goosey Loosey.

"Of course!" said Henny Penny. "But we must hurry."

As Henny Penny, Cocky Locky, Ducky Lucky, and Goosey Loosey hurried along together they met Turkey Lurkey. "Where are you going?" he asked.

"The sky is falling. We must go and tell the king," said Henny Penny.

"Oh my! Oh my! Let me come with you," said Turkey Lurkey.

"Of course!" said Henny Penny. "But we must hurry."

So Henny Penny, Cocky Locky, Ducky Lucky, Goosey Loosey, and Turkey Lurkey hurried along together, until they saw something that made them stop very suddenly. There, in their pathway, stood Foxy Loxy. "Where are you going, my fine feathered friends?" asked Foxy Loxy. (**Ask:** *Now what will happen? Do you think Foxy Loxy will want to help the animals go and tell the king?*)

"The sky is falling. We must go and tell the king," said Henny Penny, her voice trembling just a little.

"Hmm, you're going the wrong way," Foxy Loxy said slyly. "Come with me. *I* will show you a shortcut to the king!" (**Say:** *Hmmm! Do you think Foxy Loxy really has a shortcut? What does he have in mind?*)

So they all hurried along behind Foxy Loxy. Soon they came to a door. "Down here," said the fox. "Who will go first?"

Now this was the door to Foxy Loxy's den where he had planned all along to trap Henny Penny, Cocky Locky, Ducky Lucky, Goosey Loosey, and Turkey Lurkey and to gobble them up for a very fine dinner! (**Say:** *Oh, no. Now Henny and her friends have a new problem. What is it?*)

Henny Penny hesitated at the door but went on in, and guess who followed her. That's right, Cocky Locky, Ducky Lucky, Goosey Loosey, and Turkey Lurkey. When all were inside, Foxy Loxy slammed the door to keep them in while he ran to fetch some firewood for his stove. "Yum! All those roasted birds will taste delicious," he thought.

But Foxy Loxy had forgotten that he left his back door wide open that day. And by now Henny and her friends had figured out that there was no shortcut. They knew that sly Foxy Loxy planned to catch them and maybe even eat them! They were getting frightened and wondering out loud what they should do when Henny spied the open back door. "This way!" she called. "But we must hurry."

So out the back door went Henny Penny, Cocky Locky, Ducky Lucky, Goosey Loosey, and Turkey Lurkey, as fast as they could go.

And Foxy Loxy was left standing at his back door watching his dinner run flapping and squawking into the distance.

As for the sky, it is still up there where it should be. And no one ever did tell the king that it was falling—because it wasn't! The something that landed plunk! on Henny Penny's head was just a stick or a berry. Do you think Henny Penny ever figured that out? (**Ask:** *How did the animals solve their problem with the fox? Was this a happy ending?*)

Teacher Read Aloud

★LA.A.1.1.2.K.2, 3, 5

Phonemic Awareness

✔ Beginning Sound

OBJECTIVES

Children

- identify pictures whose names begin with /d/, /j/, /n/, and /w/

MATERIALS

- **Alphafriend Cards** *Dudley Duck, Jumping Jill, Nyle Noodle, Willy Worm*
- **Alphafriend Audiotapes** Theme 3, 7, 9, 10
- **Alphafolder** *Jumping Jill*
- **Picture Cards** for *d, j, n, w,* and *y*
- **Phonics Center:** Theme 10, Week 3, Day 1

Home Connection

For parents who would like to review the Alphafriends' songs with their children, **take-home versions** are on the **Alphafriends Blackline Masters.**

English Language Learners

★LA.A.1.1.2.K.2, 3, 5

Before the Compare and Review activity, have English language learners work with a fluent speaker to practice these sounds, using picture cards. The English-speaking children can help less proficient partners with the sounds and with words they may not know.

▶ Revisiting Alphafriends

Use this Alphafriend routine to review *Jumping Jill's* sound.

1 **Alphafriend Riddle** Read the clues.

  - *This Alphafriend's sound is /j/. Say it with me: /j/.*

  - *She just loves to jjjump and tell jokes.*

Say more words that begin with /j/ and call on children until they guess *Jumping Jill.*

2 **Pocket Chart** Display Jumping Jill in a pocket chart. Say her name, emphasizing the initial sound slightly, and have children echo the sound.

3 📼 **Alphafriend Audiotape** Play Jumping Jill's song, or read it from the **Alphafriends Blackline Master.** *Listen for words that begin with /j/.*

4 **Alphafolder** Have children look at the scene and name the /j/ pictures.

5 **Summarize**

  - *What is this Alphafriend's name? What is her sound?*

  - *What words in our Alphafriend's Song start with /j/?*

  - *Each time you look at Jumping Jill, remember /j/.*

6 Repeat this routine for the other Alphafriends listed in *Materials.* Use the clues below.

  - for Dudley: *This animal dives and dips in water.*

  - for Nyle: *This friend wears a napkin around his neck.*

  - for Willy: *Our wiggly friend's name is short for William.*

Jumping Jill
(Tune: "Twinkle, Twinkle, Little Star")

Jumping Jill can jump
   so high.
Jill can jump in warm July.
Jumping Jill can jump
   so low.
Jill can jump for joy,
   you know.
Join her in a jumping game.
As you jump, call out her name!

Sunshine State Standards pp. T122–T123   ★ = FCAT Benchmark in Gr. 3–5

★**LA.A.1.1.2.K.2** knows alphabet
★**LA.A.1.1.2.K.3** knows sounds of alphabet
★**LA.A.1.1.2.K.5** basic phonetic principles

▶ Listening for / d /, / j /, / n /, / w /

Compare and Review Display the four Alphafriends. Then draw Picture Cards in random order and name them. For each one, children should think of the Alphafriend whose name begins with the same sound. Choose someone to put the card below that Alphafriend. Explain that there are some "yippee" pictures that do not belong in the game; for those words, children should yell "Yippee!" and name the initial sound. Monitor responses closely to determine the need for extra instruction.

Picture Cards: *watch, doll, nine, yak, jeep, nose, well, desk, yarn, jet, nut, dot, web, yolk, net*

Practice Book p. 306

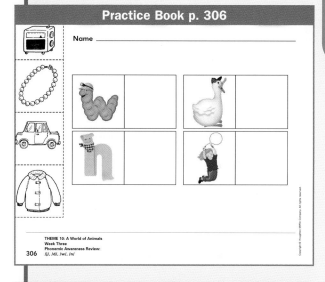

Practice Book p. 305

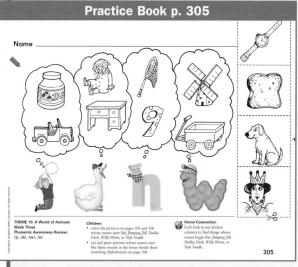

▶ Apply

Practice Book pages 305–306 Children will complete the pages at small group time.

★LA.A.1.1.2.K.2, 3, 5

At Group Time

Phonics Center

Use the Phonics Center materials for **Theme 10, Week 3, Day 1**.

★LA.A.1.1.3.K.1
LA.B.2.1.2.K.1

High-Frequency Word Practice

▶ Matching Words

■ Distribute the Word Cards. Have children read their words and match them to the same ones on the Word Wall. Then shuffle the cards and continue until everyone has a turn.

■ Have each child write his or her name on an index card as you build these sentences in the pocket chart.

_____ said she can play here.

_____ said he can play here.

■ Have children read the sentences with you. Then children can take turns putting their own name cards in the appropriate sentences and calling on classmates to read the line.

 Writing Opportunity Place the Word Cards *he, she, said, can, here, and, I,* and *play* in the pocket chart. Provide a list of class names. Children can write sentences about playing with friends, using their own names and names from the list. Then children can illustrate their sentences.

Here is Aki.
Aki said he and I can play.

Challenge

★LA.A.1.1.3.K.1

By now some children will recognize classmates' names in print. Vary the sentence-building activity by shuffling and distributing the cards with children's names. Volunteers can complete the sentence with someone else's name and challenge others to read the sentence.

English Language Learners

★LA.A.1.1.3.K.4

Help learners distinguish between *he* and *she*, by posting a picture of a boy by the word *he* and a picture of a girl by the word *she*. Say a sentence using a girl's name. Children repeat the sentence, substituting *she* for the girl's name. Repeat with a boy's name and *he.*

Sunshine State Standards pp. T124–T125   ★ = FCAT Benchmark in Gr. 3–5

★LA.A.1.1.3.K.1 identifies high-frequency words   LA.B.1.1.2.K.3 able to sequence events
★LA.A.1.1.3.K.4 uses sources to build vocabulary   LA.B.2.1.2.K.1 writes with pictures, words
★LA.E.1.1.2.K.1 sequence of events, setting   LA.E.2.1.1.K.2 uses personal interpretations

Oral Language

*LA.E.1.1.2.K.1

▶ Using Order Words

Display the circle organizer you made for *Henny Penny*, adding pictures from **Blackline Master 153** if you have not yet done so.

Ask children what they would do if they wanted to tell a friend about this story. How could they organize the events so that someone else would understand what happened? Get children's ideas, reminding them of order words, if necessary.

■ Write *1, 2, 3, 4* on the board, followed by the words *first, next, then,* and *finally*.

■ On a chart write *First*. Have children tell what happened first in the story. Write their sentence. Ask how it should begin (with a capital letter) and end (period).

■ Add *Next* to the chart, and help children decide on a way to summarize the names of all the characters who went with Henny Penny to warn the king. Explain that the exact names of all the characters are not needed in a quick summary.

■ Add *Then,* and help children develop a sentence for this part of the story. Do the same for the last or final event.

■ Read the final, sequenced summary for children.

At Group Time

Writing Center

LA.B.2.1.2.K.1
LA.E.2.1.1.K.2
LA.B.1.1.2.K.3

Hang the chart from the previous activity in the Writing Center. Highlight the order words in bright colors. Provide large sheets of paper folded to make four-page books. Children can copy the order words and illustrate the events in the story.

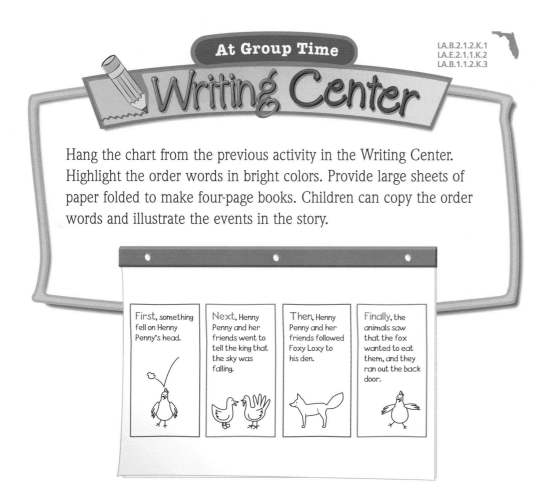

First, something fell on Henny Penny's head.

Next, Henny Penny and her friends went to tell the king that the sky was falling.

Then, Henny Penny and her friends followed Foxy Loxy to his den.

Finally, the animals saw that the fox wanted to eat them, and they ran out the back door.

Day 2

Day at a Glance

Learning to Read

Big Book:

Splash!

☑ **Phonics:**
*Initial
Consonants* **j,
d, w, n,**
page T130

☑ **High-Frequency Word Review:**
are, he, page T132

Word Work

High-Frequency Word Practice,
page T134

Writing & Language

Vocabulary Expansion, *page T135*

Managing Small Groups

Teacher-Led Group
• Begin *Practice Book,* 160 or 186, 307–308
  and **Blackline Masters** 166 or 192.

Independent Groups
• Finish *Practice Book,* 170 or 196, 307–308
  and **Blackline Masters** 179 or 205.
• Phonics Center: Theme 10, Week 3, Day 2
• Book, other Centers

Opening

LA.A.2.1.5.K.2
★LA.A.1.1.2.K.6
★LA.A.1.1.3.K.4

Calendar

Sunday	Monday	Tuesday	Wednesday	Thursday	Friday	Saturday
			1	2	3	4
5	6	7	8	9	10	11
12	13	14	15	16	17	18
19	20	21	22	23	24	25
26	27	28	29	30	31	

Chant the days of the week with children, using order words: *First comes Sunday; next comes Monday; then comes Tuesday, Wednesday, Thursday, and Friday. Last comes Saturday!*

Daily Message

Interactive Writing Have children use order words to describe the plans for the day. Call on children occasionally to write an initial capital letter or add appropriate punctuation.

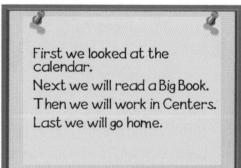

First we looked at the calendar.
Next we will read a Big Book.
Then we will work in Centers.
Last we will go home.

Word Wall

Play "Pass the Pointer." Children can take turns finding Word Wall words with a pointer as you call them out.

★LA.A.1.1.2.K.5
LA.C.1.1.4.K.1

 ## Daily Phonemic Awareness
Blending and Segmenting Phonemes

Explain that when the king heard about the Foxy Loxy's trick on Henny Penny, he would not let Foxy visit the castle. **You** *may visit, though, if you say the code words. Listen: / s / / k / / ī /. What is the word?* (sky)

- Continue, having children blend sounds to get the words *nut, head, hen, goose,* and *run.*

- Now reverse the game, asking children for the separate "code sounds" in these words: *chick, cat, den, code.*

 ## Phoneme Substitution

- *Sometimes the king makes the code word really hard by asking you to change a sound. Change the / k / in* cat *to / m /.* (mat) Continue, asking children to change the / h / in *hen* to / p / (pen); the / n / in *nut* to / k / (cut).

Sunshine State Standards pp. T126–T127
★ = FCAT Benchmark in Gr. 3–5

★**LA.A.1.1.2.K.5** basic phonetic principles
★**LA.A.1.1.2.K.6** print conveys meaning
★**LA.A.1.1.3.K.4** uses sources to build vocabulary
LA.A.2.1.5.K.2 pictures, signs for information
LA.C.1.1.4.K.1 listens for specific information

Getting Ready to Learn

To help plan their day, tell children that they will

- revisit the Big Book *Splash!*

- review the letters *Dd, Jj, Nn, Ww* and their sounds.

- read and learn more about animals around the world in the Book Center.

DAY 2

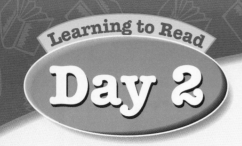
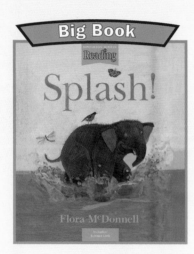

Big Book

Reading

Splash!

Flora McDonnell

Purposes • concepts of print • story language • reading strategy • comprehension skill

LA.C.1.1.1.K.2 ★LA.A.2.1.1.K.1
LA.A.1.1.1.K.1 LA.A.1.1.4.K.1
LA.C.1.1.4.K.1 ★LA.A.1.1.2.K.5
★LA.E.1.1.2.K.1 LA.E.2.1.1.K.2

Sharing the Big Book
Oral Language/Comprehension

▶ **Building Background**

Display *Splash!* Call on volunteers to share what they remember about it. Tell children that as you reread the story, they should look for the important events.

Strategy:

Summarize

Teacher-Student Modeling Remind children that thinking about the most important parts of a story can help them retell it.

As we read this again, let's think about how we could use our own words to tell someone else about the story.

 Comprehension Focus:
Story Structure: Plot

Teacher-Student Modeling Remind children that a story is made up of important happenings including the characters' problem and the way they solve it. *These events are told in an order that makes sense. In this story, what important thing happened first? What was the animals' problem? Thinking about their problem and how they solved it later will help us retell the story in our own words.*

Extra Support

★LA.E.1.1.2.K.1

If children have difficulty telling the plot (problem, solution), look through a familiar fairy tale with them. Model telling the important events, and then ask children to do the same in their own words.

 Sunshine State Standards pp. T128–T129   ★ = FCAT Benchmark in Gr. 3–5

★**LA.A.1.1.2.K.1** how print is organized
★**LA.A.1.1.2.K.5** basic phonetic principles
★**LA.A.2.1.1.K.1** main idea from a read-aloud
★**LA.E.1.1.2.K.1** sequence of events, setting
LA.A.1.1.1.K.1 oral predictions
LA.A.1.1.4.K.1 strategies to comprehend text

▶ Sharing the Story

Reread the story, pausing for these discussion points.

 pages 2–10

Story Structure: Plot

- *What problems does the heat cause for the animals? Who helps them? How will going to the water solve their problems?*

pages 10–13

Noting Important Details

- *What things in the art make this story more interesting or funny?*

pages 13–19

Strategy: Summarize

- *We said the animals were hot at the beginning. Then the baby elephant led them to the water. Now you finish telling what happens.* (Example: The animals play in the water. It cools them off and makes them happy.)

 page 22

Concepts of Print: Beginning and End of a Sentence

- *Who will point to the first word in the first sentence? in the second one? How does the first word always start?* (capital letter) *Point to the end of the first sentence. How do you know where it ends?*

▶ Responding

Role Playing Have partners show how the baby elephant led the others without speaking.

 **At Group Time**

 **Book Center**

LA.A.2.1.2.K.1

Add more books about animals to your Book Center for children to compare: nonfiction books with photographs, storybooks with illustrations, and books with several habitats. (See pages iv-v.)

 Challenge

★LA.A.1.1.2.K.1

Write the animal names on index cards. Children can go through the story and clip their cards to pages with pictures of those animals.

 English Language Learners

LA.A.1.1.4.K.1

Encourage learners to talk about the story by asking questions and prompting them to use the pictures to answer them. Start with yes-no or multiple-choice questions before moving into *wh-* questions. Then help children use the pictures to retell the story.

Sharing the Big Book (T129)

LA.A.2.1.2.K.1 reads for pleasure
LA.C.1.1.1.K.2 listens to oral language
LA.C.1.1.4.K.1 listens for specific information
LA.E.2.1.1.K.2 uses personal interpretations

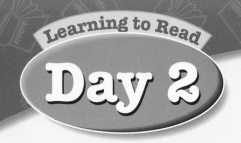
★LA.A.1.1.2.K.2, 3, 5
★LA.A.1.1.2.K.3

Phonics

✓ Initial Consonants d, j, n, and w

▶ Develop Phonemic Awareness

Beginning Sound Play a listening game. Tell children you will say some words and they should take one step forward if they hear / d / at the *beginning* of a word. During play some children may respond for a word with *final* / d /; discuss the sound's position and tell children they must listen carefully! Words: *dog, deer, box, do, lid, work, dip, donkey, goat, door.* Play again, this time with initial / n /: *nose, not, nest, pan, let, noodle, joke, watch, number, nail, wing.*

▶ Connect Sounds to Letters

Beginning Letter *What letter stands for the sound / j /, as in* jump? *What character will help you remember the sound for* j? Display *Jumping Jill* and have children name the letter.

Repeat this routine with *Dudley Duck, Nyle Noodle,* and *Willy Worm.*

Now tell children you want to write *nest* on the board. *What letter should I write first? How do you know?* Write *nest,* and then repeat with the words *west, deep,* and *jeep.*

Compare and Review: d, j, n, w In the pocket chart, display the Letter Cards as shown and the Picture Cards in random order. In turn, children can name a picture, say the beginning sound, and put the card below the right letter.

Extra Support

If the letter name *w* leads children to associate it with / d /, explain that this letter's name does not give a clue to its sound. Have children trace *w* in sand, saying the / w / sound with each stroke.

Sunshine State Standards pp. T130–T131   ★ = FCAT Benchmark in Gr. 3–5

★LA.A.1.1.2.K.2 knows alphabet
★LA.A.1.1.2.K.3 knows sounds of alphabet
★LA.A.1.1.2.K.5 basic phonetic principles

▶ Handwriting

Writing D, d, J, j, N, n, W, w Tell children that now they'll practice writing the letters that stand for the sounds they've been working with. Stand at the board and write a capital *J* with your finger, asking children to copy your movements and trace the letter in the air.

What letter did we write? How do you know? Have several children write that letter with chalk. Then continue with the other letters.

▶ Apply

Practice Book page 307 Children will complete the page at small group time.

Blackline Masters 160, 166, 170, 179 These pages provide additional handwriting practice for small group time.

At Group Time

Phonics Center

★LA.A.1.1.2.K.2, 3, 5

Use the Phonics Center materials for **Theme 10, Week 3, Day 2.**

Practice Book p. 307

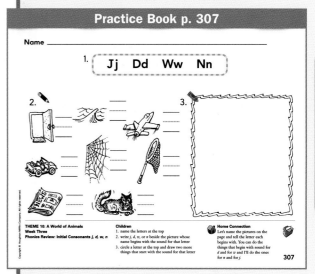

Name _____

1. Jj Dd Ww Nn

Portfolio Opportunity

Save the **Practice Book** page to show children's grasp of the letter-sound associations.

Save the **Blackline Masters** for end-of-year handwriting samples.

Learning to Read
Day 2

 High-Frequency Words

Review Words: are, he

OBJECTIVES

Children

- read and write the high-frequency words *are* and *he*

MATERIALS

- **Word Cards** *and, are, He, he, Here, here, I, Is, is, play*
- **Punctuation Cards:** period, question mark
- ***Higglety Pigglety: A Book of Rhymes,*** page 7

Teacher's Note

Prepare the word cards *Can, can* for the sentence-building activity.

▶ **Teach**

Tell children that today they will practice reading and writing two words that they will see often in stories. Say *he* and call on volunteers to use the word in context.

Write *he* on the board. Then lead children in a chant, clapping on each beat, to help them remember the spelling: **h-e, he! h-e, he!**

Repeat for the word *are*.

Word Wall Have children find *he* and *are* on the Word Wall, and remind them to look there when they need to remember how to write the words.

▶ **Practice**

Reading Build sentences in the pocket chart as shown. Children take turns reading the sentences aloud. Place the pocket chart in the **Phonics Center** along with extra cards for *can, is,* and *she* so that children can practice building and reading their own sentences.

Sunshine State Standards pp. T132–T133   ★ = FCAT Benchmark in Gr. 3–5

★**LA.A.1.1.3.K.1** identifies high-frequency words
★**LA.A.1.1.3.K.4** uses sources to build vocabulary

- Play a matching game. Reread "Crackers and Crumbs" on page 7 of *Higglety Pigglety*. Have children hold up Word Cards for *are* every time they hear the word. Then read the poem again, tracking the print. Have children take turns matching the word *are* on their cards to the word *are* in the poem.

Higglety Pigglety: A Book of Rhymes, page 7

- Write the following rhyme on chart paper and continue the activity with the word *he:*

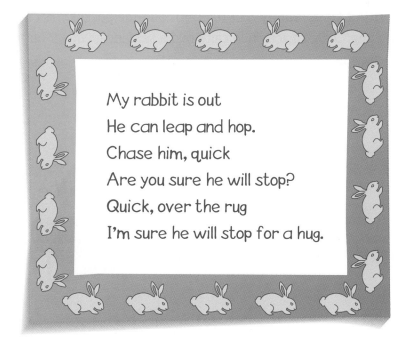

My rabbit is out
He can leap and hop.
Chase him, quick
Are you sure he will stop?
Quick, over the rug
I'm sure he will stop for a hug.

▶ **Apply**

Practice Book page 308 Children will read and write *are* and *he* as they complete the **Practice Book** page. On Day 3, they will practice reading those words in the **Phonics Library** story "The Bug Hut."

Practice Book p. 308

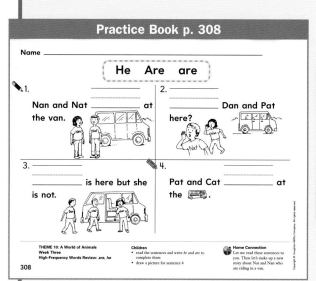

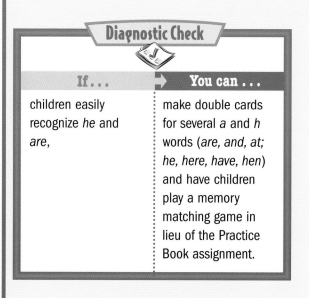

Diagnostic Check

If . . .	You can . . .
children easily recognize *he* and *are*,	make double cards for several *a* and *h* words (*are, and, at; he, here, have, hen*) and have children play a memory matching game in lieu of the Practice Book assignment.

★LA.A.1.1.3.K.1
LA.B.2.1.2.K.1

High-Frequency Word Practice

▶ Building Sentences

Tell children that you want them to help you build sentences about animals. Display the Word Cards.

- *I want the first word to be A. Who will find it and put it in the pocket chart? Should it be spelled with a capital A or a small a? Why?*

- Continue, having children build the sentence *A [zebra] is at the [zoo].* Then scramble the words and choose children to build the sentence again.

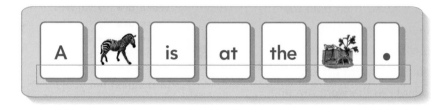

- To extend the activity, display pictures of assorted animals and locales. Children can take turns building and reading new sentences about animals.

✏ **Writing Opportunity** Put the cards and the pocket chart in the Writing Center. Each child can build a sentence, copy it onto art paper, and add a drawing.

OBJECTIVES

Children

- read high-frequency words
- create and write sentences with high-frequency words

MATERIALS

- **Word Cards** *A, a, is, The, the*
- **Punctuation Card:** period
- **Picture Cards** *zebra, zoo,* other animal cards

📎 Teacher's Note

Prepare the word card *at* for this activity. To extend the activity with sentences about other environments, make your own picture cards for a forest, a jungle, a pond, and a desert, and use appropriate animal pictures.

Sunshine State Standards pp. T134–T135   ★ = FCAT Benchmark in Gr. 3–5

★**LA.A.1.1.3.K.1** identifies high-frequency words   ★**LA.A.1.1.3.K.4** uses sources to build vocabulary
★**LA.A.1.1.3.K.3** sorts words from categories   **LA.B.2.1.2.K.1** writes with pictures, words

Vocabulary Expansion

▶ Animal Names

Viewing Together, look through *Splash!* and name the animals. Point out that the book is about *wild* animals, and ask if those animals would make good pets.

Now look through *Which Pet?* and compare the animals to the ones in *Splash!* Ask why these animals make better pets.

Help children brainstorm a list of animals that people may have as pets. Choose a few children to look through *Which Pet?* and other appropriate picture books for more ideas.

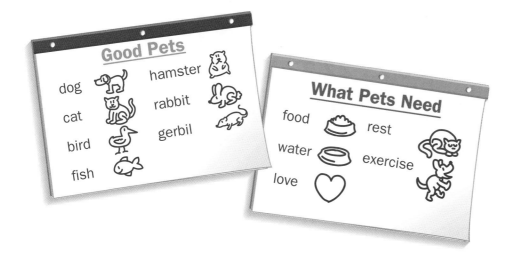

On a separate chart, list things pets need. Talk about some of the animals on the first list for ideas.

Tell children that tomorrow they will use the lists to help them write about how to take care of a pet.

OBJECTIVES

Children
- brainstorm lists of pets and their needs

MATERIALS
- **Big Books:** *Splash!, Which Pet?*

Day at a Glance

Learning to Read

Big Book:

Feathers for Lunch

 Phonics:
Blending *-ug*
and *-ut* Words
(*bug, cut*),
page T140

Word Work

Building Words, *page T142*

Writing & Language

Shared Writing, *page T143*

Managing Small Groups

Teacher-Led Group
- Read **Phonics Library** selection "The Bug Hut."
- Write letters *U/u; begin* **Blackline Masters 177 or 203.**
- Begin *Practice Book, 309–310.*

Independent Groups
- Finish **Blackline Masters 177 or 203** and *Practice Book, 309–310.*
- Math, other Centers

Opening

LA.A.2.1.5.K.2
★LA.A.1.1.2.K.6
★LA.A.1.1.3.K.4

Calendar

Sunday	Monday	Tuesday	Wednesday	Thursday	Friday	Saturday
			1	2	3	4
5	6	7	8	9	10	11
12	13	14	15	16	17	18
19	20	21	22	23	24	25
26	27	28	29	30	31	

Point to the month and date on the calendar. Have children tell what day it is. Note that *May* and *day* (or *June* and *moon*) rhyme. Help children brainstorm other words that rhyme with the name of the month.

Daily Message

Interactive Writing You might write your thoughts about the literature. Have children help write the beginning consonants of the words in the message. Then read the message, and add a few sentences about the children's opinions.

Miss Swanson's favorite author is Lois Ehlert. She thinks the colors are great!

Play "Rhyme Time." *I'm thinking of an action word for something you like to do. It rhymes with* May *and* day. *What word is it?* (play) Continue with rhyming clues for other words.

✓ Daily Phonemic Awareness
Blending and Segmenting Phonemes

Read "Peter Piper" on page 23 of *Higglety Pigglety*.

- *What is this word from the poem? Put these sounds together: /p//ĕ/ /k/. What word it that?* (peck) *Now guess the names of other things you might pick in a garden.* Continue with *bean, peach,* and *yam.*

- Next, have children segment the phonemes in: *hose, rake, pot.*

✓ Phoneme Substitution

- *Now listen to the word rose. If I change the first sound from /r/ to /n/, what word do I have?* (nose) *If I change the last sound from /z/ to /t/, what word is that?* (note) *If I change the first letter to /g/, what do I have?* (goat)

- Invite children to make the poem sillier by substituting /m/ for /p/, and saying the rhyme: *Meter Miper micked a meck ...*

Peter Piper

Peter Piper picked a peck
   of pickled peppers.
A peck of pickled peppers
   Peter Piper picked.
If Peter Piper picked a peck
   of pickled peppers,
Where's the peck of pickled peppers
Peter Piper picked?

a Tongue Twister

23

Higglety Pigglety: A Book of Rhymes, page 23

DAY 3

Getting Ready to Learn

To help plan their day, tell children that they will

- listen to the Big Book *Feathers for Lunch.*

- read a story called "The Bug Hut."

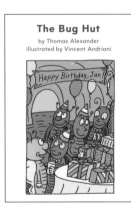

- make bird and cat puppets with shapes in the Math Center.

LA.C.1.1.1.K.2   LA.E.1.1.2.K.1
LA.A.1.1.1.K.1   ★LA.E.1.1.2.K.1
LA.A.1.1.4.K.1   ★LA.A.1.1.2.K.1, 4

Sharing the Big Book
Oral Language/Comprehension

▶ Building Background

Display *Feathers for Lunch.* Have children share what they remember about this story. Explain that children will hear the story again, enjoy the colorful pictures, and look for the *JINGLES* and birdcalls!

Strategy: Summarize

Student Modeling *If you want to tell someone else about this story, what should you think about as we reread this story? What will that help you do?*

Comprehension Focus:
Story Structure: Plot

Student Modeling *What are the important parts of this story? Where in the story do you usually learn about the problem? Where in the story can you usually find the solution?*

Big Book

HOUGHTON MIFFLIN
Reading

Feathers for Lunch

Lois Ehlert

Includes:
Science Link

Purposes • concepts of print • story language
• reading strategy • comprehension skill

Extra Support

LA.C.2.1.1.K.1
★LA.E.1.1.2.K.1

Help children understand the problem and solution by discussing the nature of cats and pointing out the words *JINGLE JINGLE* and the birdcalls in the illustrations.

English Language Learners

LA.A.1.1.4.K.1

Draw a story map, including *characters, problem, solution.* Ask learners questions to supply information. Fill in the map. Help children use the information from the map to make sentences. Write their sentences. Point out that these sentences are a *summary* of the story.

Sunshine State Standards pp. T138–T139   ★ = FCAT Benchmark in Gr. 3–5

★**LA.A.1.1.2.K.1** how print is organized   **LA.A.1.1.1.K.1** oral predictions
★**LA.A.1.1.2.K.4** concept of words, meaning   **LA.A.1.1.4.K.1** strategies to comprehend text
★**LA.E.1.1.2.K.1** sequence of events, setting **LA.C.1.1.1.K.2** listens to oral language

▶ Sharing the Story

Reread the story, pausing for these discussion points:

✓ page 3
Concepts of Print: Beginning and End of a Sentence

■ *What clues tell you which is the first word of the sentence? What clue shows you the end of the sentence? When would you see a question mark?*

✓ pages 4–15
Story Structure: Plot

■ *What problem does the cat have? What is he trying to do in the story?*
(He's hungry, and he wants to catch a wild bird for lunch.)

✓ pages 20–27
Story Structure: Plot

■ *Does the cat ever solve his problem?* (He never catches a bird. His owner catches him and probably feeds him lunch.) *Do you think the cat will try to catch birds again? Explain.*

▶ Responding

Summarize Help children develop pictures about the plot (events, problem, solution) and use them to summarize the story in their own words.

Practice Book page 309 Children complete the page at small group time.

At Group Time
MA.C.1.1.1

Math Center

Materials • paper • crayons or markers • glue • craft sticks • feathers

Have children create birds and cats with paper cut into ovals, circles, and triangles. Children glue the shapes onto craft sticks to make puppets.

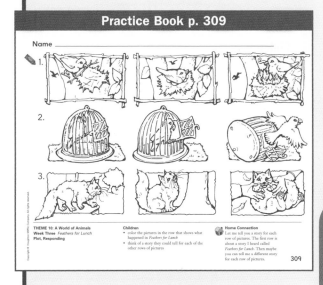

Practice Book p. 309

Name _____

DAY 3

📎 Teacher's Note

You may wish to make a list of birds children have seen outside—either at home, on trips, or at school. Post this in the Writing Center along with bird guides to encourage children to write about birds.

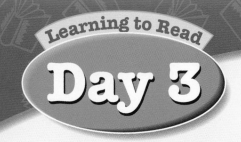

★LA.A.1.1.2.K.2, 3, 5
★LA.A.1.1.3.K.4

Phonics

✅ Blending -ug and -ut Words

▶ Connect Sounds to Letters

Review Consonant *b* Play Benny Bear's song, and have children clap for each /b/ word. Write B and *b* on the board, and list words from the song.

Blending -*ug* Words Build the word *bug* letter by letter as you say the sounds. Take away the *b* and hold up the Letter Card *t*. Put *t* in front of -*ug*, and ask children to blend the new word. (tug) Have volunteers blend the word and point. Ask children what letters they would choose to build *dug, lug, mug,* and *rug*. Have children blend as you point.

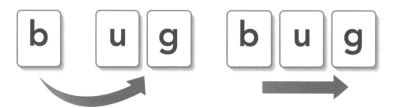

Blending -*ut* Words Follow the same procedure to build *cut, but, hut, jut, nut,* and *rut*. Have children blend as you point.

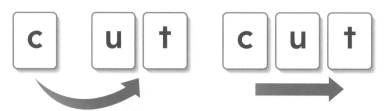

 Point out *bug* and *cut* on the Word Wall.

▶ Apply

Practice Book page 310 Children complete the page at small group time.

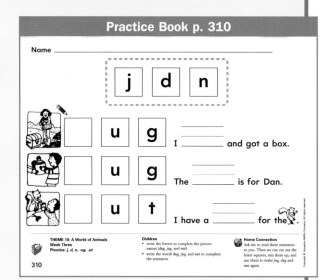

Practice Book p. 310

Sunshine State Standards pp. T140–T141   ★ = FCAT Benchmark in Gr. 3–5

★**LA.A.1.1.2.K.2** knows alphabet   ★**LA.A.1.1.3.K.1** identifies high-frequency words
★**LA.A.1.1.2.K.3** knows sounds of alphabet   ★**LA.A.1.1.3.K.4** uses sources to build vocabulary
★**LA.A.1.1.2.K.5** basic phonetic principles

Reading
Phonics Library

A World of Animals

Reading

Look at the first picture together. Make sure children understand that the bugs are giving a birthday party for Jan at a restaurant called *The Bug Hut*.

Phonics/Decoding Strategy

Teacher-Student Modeling Discuss using the Strategy to read words in the story.

Think Aloud

What is the first word in the title of this book? (The) *The next word in the title begins with capital B. The sound for B is / b /. We know the sounds for u, g:/ ŭ /,/ g /, -ug. Blend the sounds.* (/ b // ug /, Bug) *We know the sounds for the next word too:/ h // ŭ // t /. Who will blend the sounds?* (Hut) *Now read the title.* (The Bug Hut) *Does the title* The Bug Hut *make sense for a story about bugs?*

Have children read the title silently. Then ask volunteers to model how they blended the words

▶ Coached Reading

Have children read each page silently before reading with you. Prompts:

page 18   *Put your finger on the word that tells what Big Bug can do.* (lug) Have volunteers model how they blended *lug.*

page 20   Together, blend *hug.* Ask: *What other words here rhyme with* hug? (Bug) *What letters are the same in those rhyming words?* (u, g) *Why can't Jan Bug jig?* (Her leg is in a cast.)

pages 21–22 *Who will read what the bugs can do?*

page 23   *Who will read what Jan Bug can do?* Have volunteers model how they blended the last sentence. *How do Jan's friends help? Do you think Jan Bug had a happy birthday?*

Purposes
• apply phonics skills
• apply high-frequency words

The Bug Hut
by Thomas Alexander
illustrated by Vincent Andriani

17

Big Bug can lug a fat box.

Dot Bug got a hat.

18   19

Here is Jan Bug.
Hug, hug, hug!

Big Bug can jig.
Dot Bug can jig.

20   21

But Jan Bug can not jig.

She CAN jig!
Jan Bug can jig, jig, jig.

22   23

DAY 3

Home Connection

Children can color the pictures in the take-home version of "The Bug Hut." After reading on Day 4, they can take it home to read to family members.

Day 3

★LA.A.1.1.2.K.5
★LA.A.1.1.3.K.4

Building Words

▶ Word Families: -*ug, -ut*

■ Tell children you want to build the word *hug*, using the Letter Cards. ***Hold up fingers to tell me how many sounds you hear in*** hug. ***Raise your hand when you know what letters I need to build the word*** hug. ***What letters should I choose?***

■ ***Now what happens if I change*** h ***to*** d? ***Read the new word.*** (*dug*) ***Now, who can make*** jug? lug? mug? rug? tug?

■ ***Now we'll change*** rug ***to*** rut. ***What letter do you hear at the end of*** rut? (*t*) ***Who will put that in place?*** Continue with *but, cut, hut, jut,* and *nut.*

■ ***Now think of a word with*** -ug ***or*** -ut. ***In just a minute, I'll ask you to whisper it to a partner. Then I'll ask someone to come to the pocket chart and build it. We'll all read the word you made.***

Have small groups play a game building -*ug* and -*ut* words. Children sit in a circle. They begin with a word card for *bug*. As the card is passed around the circle, each child puts a self-stick note over the initial consonant and writes another letter to create a new word. The player reads the word aloud. When the *bug* card gets back to the first player, a word card for *cut* is used for the next round. Children can vary the game by substituting ending rather than beginning consonants.

Sunshine State Standards pp. T142–T143   ★ = FCAT Benchmark in Gr. 3–5

★**LA.A.1.1.2.K.5** basic phonetic principles   **LA.B.1.1.2.K.3** able to sequence events
★**LA.A.1.1.3.K.4** uses sources to build vocabulary   **LA.C.1.1.1.K.1** follows 2-step oral directions
LA.B.1.1.2.K.1 dictates messages

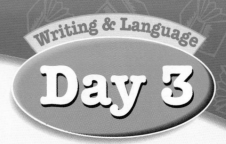
Shared Writing

LA.B.1.1.2.K.1, 3
LA.C.1.1.1.K.1

▶ **Writing Directions**

Listening, Speaking, and Viewing Remind children how they use order words to help readers know when things happen in their writing.

■ Review the Link *Which Pet?* and the list of pets you developed in yesterday's writing activity. (See page T135.)

■ Ask children to choose a pet to write about. Explain that they will be writing directions on how to care for this pet. Vote on their favorite one.

■ Label a piece of chart paper "How to Care for a (fill in the chosen pet)."

■ Write children's suggestions for chores to do and equipment needed for this pet.

■ Have children evaluate what they have done. Have they included the most important parts? Is there anything they need to add?

■ Ask children, *Does the order of the sentences make sense? Which sentence should go first?* Number the sentences according to what the group decides.

■ Rewrite the sentences in order, adding the words *first, next, then,* and *finally.*

■ Show children as you read the chart how you wrote a capital letter at the beginning of each sentence and how you put a punctuation mark at the end.

How to Care for a Fish

First, you need a bowl or a tank.

Next, you need to fill it with clean water.

Then, you put the fish in it.

Finally, you need to feed the fish every day.

OBJECTIVES

Children
• think of sentences to contribute to a list of directions

MATERIALS

• **Big Book:** *Which Pet?*

DAY 3

English Language Learners

LA.B.1.1.2.K.1, 3
LA.C.1.1.1.K.1

Choose a familiar class activity, such as getting ready for lunch. Have learners pretend they are giving directions to new classmates. As they tell you what to do first, next, then, and last, have a child demonstrate each action. Write the directions on chart paper and read them for children.

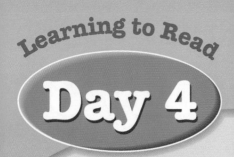

Day 4

Day at a Glance

Learning to Read

Big Book Links:

Baby Animals Play, Which Pet?

☑ **Phonics:** Reviewing Consonant *j* ; Blending *-ug* and *-ut* Words, *page T148*

Word Work

Building Words, *page T150*

Writing & Language

Interactive Writing, *page T151*

Managing Small Groups

Teacher-Led Group
- Reread *Phonics Library* selection "The Bug Hut."
- Begin *Practice Book*, 311.

Independent Groups
- Finish *Practice Book*, 311.
- Phonics Center: Theme 10, Week 3, Day 4
- Writing, other Centers

Opening

LA.A.2.1.5.K.2
★LA.A.1.1.2.K.6
★LA.A.1.1.3.K.4

Calendar

Sunday	Monday	Tuesday	Wednesday	Thursday	Friday	Saturday
			1	2	3	4
5	6	7	8	9	10	11
12	13	14	15	16	17	18
19	20	21	22	23	24	25
26	27	28	29	30	31	

Chant the days of the week a few times with children. Have them fly like birds as they chant, and "land" on a branch each Sunday.

Daily Message

Interactive Writing Ask children what baby animals they know. Have they seen the animals play? Write about how the baby animals play. Ask volunteers to contribute names, high-frequency words, letters, and punctuation to the message.

We know some baby animals!
Sarah's kittens play with string.
Jacob's puppy chases a ball.

Ask children to find the word *play* on the Word Wall. Then call on children to choose words for others to find.

★LA.A.1.1.2.K.5
LA.C.1.1.4.K.1

✓ Daily Phonemic Awareness
Blending and Segmenting Phonemes

Read "To Market, To Market" on page 31 of *Higglety Pigglety*.

- What is this word from the poem? Put these sounds together: /j//i//g/. What word is that? (jig) Have children blend phomenes in hog and bun. Then have children segment the phonemes in these words: *pig*, *fat*, *jog*.

✓ Phoneme Substitution

- Have some fun with nonsense words. **Jiggety jog.** *What if I changed the /j/ to /p/? Let's say it together:* **Piggety pog.** (Biggety Bog; Ziggety Zog).

- Play "catch" with final phonemes. Begin by saying *jig*. The next player changes the final sound to make a new word, such as *Jim*, and so on. These words are good starters: *jog (job, jot, Jon), bun (bus, bug, but)*.

Sunshine State Standards pp. T144–T145
★ = FCAT Benchmark in Gr. 3–5

★**LA.A.1.1.2.K.5** basic phonetic principles
★**LA.A.1.1.2.K.6** print conveys meaning
★**LA.A.1.1.3.K.4** uses sources to build vocabulary
LA.A.2.1.5.K.2 pictures, signs for information
LA.C.1.1.4.K.1 listens for specific information

Getting Ready to Learn

To help plan their day, tell children that they will

- reread the Science Links: *Baby Animals Play* and *Which Pet?*

- learn to make and read new words in the Phonics Center.

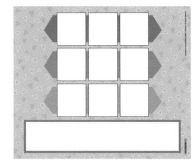

- reread a story called "The Bug Hut."

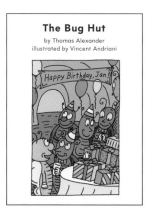

The Bug Hut
by Thomas Alexander
illustrated by Vincent Andriani

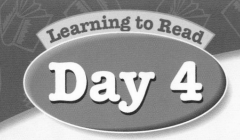
SC.F.1.1.3 ★LA.A1.1.2.K.1, 2
LA.A.1.1.1.K.1 LA.E.2.1.1.K.1
★LA.A.2.1.1.K.1 LA.A.1.1.4.K.1
FCAT Benchmark in Gr. 3–5

Sharing the Big Books

Science Link

▶ Building Background

Rereading for Understanding *You may know some baby animals. What baby animals do we see here?* Display *Baby Animals Play*, read the title, and show a few pictures. Encourage discussion. *Today let's pay special attention to the baby animals' names.* Pause for discussion as you reread.

---

pages 32–33

Strategy: Question

Student Modeling *What questions could you ask if you didn't understand these pages?* (What is a baby [specific animal]? What does this baby animal like to do?)

---

pages 32–33

Making Judgments

■ *Why do you think baby animals play? What things do they learn from playing? How might those things keep them safe?*

 page 33

Concepts of Print: Beginning and End of a Sentence

■ Read the first sentence on page 33. *Where does the sentence begin? How do you know? Where does the sentence end? How do you know? What mark is this—a period, an exclamation point, or a question mark?* Repeat with the last sentence on the page.

▶ Responding

Evaluating Encourage children to discuss what baby animals learn from playing. *How do you like to play? What do you learn from playing?*

Big Book
Baby Animals Play
Splash!
Flora McDonnell

pages 29–35

Extra Support

LA.A.1.1.1.K.1
LA.A.1.1.4.K.1

Before rereading, invite pairs of children to revisit the selections by taking picture walks through them. Children can take turns sharing what they remember, using the pictures as prompts.

Sunshine State Standards pp. T146–T147   ★ = FCAT Benchmark in Gr. 3–5

★**LA.A.1.1.2.K.1** how print is organized   LA.A.1.1.1.K.1 oral predictions
★**LA.A.1.1.2.K.2** knows alphabet   LA.A.1.1.4.K.1 strategies to comprehend text
★**LA.A.2.1.1.K.1** main idea from a read-aloud   LA.C.3.1.3.K.1 uses speaking vocabulary

Science Link

▶ Building Background

Rereading for Understanding Remind children that they also read *Which Pet?* Pause for discussion as you share this selection again.

> **pages 34–38**
>
> ### Strategy: Question
>
> **Student Modeling** *What kind of sentence is at the end of each page? Could you ask yourself that question to make sure you understand the selection?* Go through the pages together, and have children tell how the words and pictures helped them answer each question.

✓ pages 35–36
Concepts of Print: Beginning and End of a Sentence

■ Ask a child to frame the first sentence on page 35. Ask another child to find the sentence beginning and name the capital letter. Ask a third child to find and name the punctuation mark at the end. Do the same for the second sentence on page 36.

page 39
Noting Details

■ Reread page 39. *What details in the words and pictures help you answer the question?* (what the animals are; what the foods are)

▶ Responding

Compare and Contrast Have children talk about how *Baby Animals Play* and *Which Pet?* are the same and different. List some of their responses on a simple Venn diagram. Children can also talk about how these nonfiction selections differ from stories like *Splash!* and *Feathers for Lunch.*

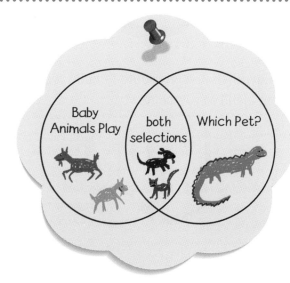

OBJECTIVES

Children
● recognize the use of a capital letter at the beginning of a sentence and a punctuation mark at the end

Big Book

HOUGHTON MIFFLIN
Reading

Feathers for Lunch

Lois

Reading
Feathers for Lunch

Lois Ehlert

pages 33–39

DAY 4

⬤ MEETING INDIVIDUAL NEEDS Challenge

LA.C.3.1.3.K.1

Some children may wish to use the Links as models for their own books. Children can state their names and tell about something they like to do.

Sharing the Big Books (T147)

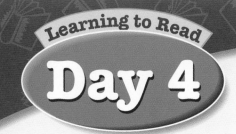

Learning to Read
Day 4

OBJECTIVES

Children

• identify initial *j* for words that begin with /j/

• blend *j* and other initial consonants with -*ug* and -*ut*

MATERIALS

• *From Apples to Zebras: A Book of ABCs* page 11

• **Alphafriend Cards** *Jumping Jill, Umbie Umbrella*

• **Letter Cards** *b, c, d, g, h, j, l, m, n, r, t, u*

• **Word Cards** *a, I, The, to*

• **Picture Card** *hut*

• **Phonics Center:** Theme 10, Week 3, Day 4

Teacher's Note

During writing, children may ask how to spell words from the -*ug* and -*ut* families. Have volunteers make a list of each set of patterned words, and hang the lists in the Writing Center.

Phonics

✔ Blending -ug and -ut Words

▶ Connect Sounds to Letters

Review Consonant *j* Using self-stick notes, cover the words on page 11 of *From Apples to Zebras: A Book of ABC's.* Display the page, asking children to name each picture and tell what letter they expect to see first in each word and why. Uncover the words so that children can check their predictions.

Reviewing -*ug* and -*ut* Review the sounds for -*ug* and -*ut*, using the appropriate Alphafriends or pages of *From Apples to Zebras* if necessary.

From Apples to Zebras: A Book of ABC's, page 11

Blending -*ug* and -*ut* Words Build the word *jug* letter by letter as you say the sounds. Take away the *j* and hold up the Letter Card m. **If we add m, what word will we have?** Put *m* in front of -*ug*, and ask children to blend the new word. *(mug)* Ask children what letters you need to build *bug, dug, hug, lug, rug,* and *tug.* Have children blend the words as you point.

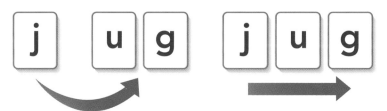

Follow the same procedure to build *jut, cut, but, hut, nut,* and *rut.* Have children blend as you point.

Sunshine State Standards pp. T148–T149   ★ = FCAT Benchmark in Gr. 3–5

★**LA.A.1.1.2.K.2** knows alphabet
★**LA.A.1.1.2.K.3** knows sounds of alphabet
★**LA.A.1.1.2.K.5** basic phonetic principles

▶ Apply

Make word cards for the decodable words *bug, ran,* and *hut,* or use the Picture Card for *hut.* Ask children to form a sentence with you: *The bug ran.* Repeat the activity to build the sentence *I ran to a hut.* Then call on volunteers to read both sentences and blend the *-ug* and *-ut* words.

Practice Book page 311 Children will complete this page at small group time.

Phonics Library In groups today, children will also read *-ug* and *-ut* words as they reread the **Phonics Library** story "The Bug Hut." See suggestions, page T141.

At Group Time
Phonics Center

★LA.A.1.1.2.K.2, 3, 5

Use the Phonics Center materials for **Theme 10, Week 3, Day 4**.

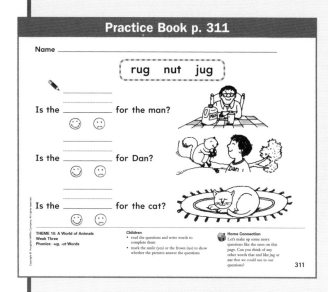

Practice Book p. 311

Name _____

rug   nut   jug

Is the _____ for the man?
☺ ☹

Is the _____ for Dan?
☺ ☹

Is the _____ for the cat?
☺ ☹

THEME 10: A World of Animals
Week Three
Phonics: -ug, -ut Words

Children
• read the questions and write words to complete them
• mark the smile (yes) or the frown (no) to show whether the pictures answer the questions

Home Connection Let's make up some more questions like the ones on this page. Can you think of any other words that end like *jug* or *nut* that we could use in our questions?

311

Diagnostic Check

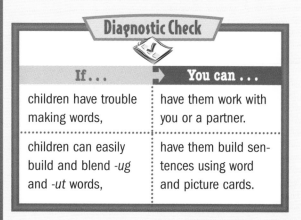

If...	You can ...
children have trouble making words,	have them work with you or a partner.
children can easily build and blend *-ug* and *-ut* words,	have them build sentences using word and picture cards.

Phonics (T149)

Day 4

OBJECTIVES

Children

- build and read *-ug* and *-ut* words

MATERIALS

- **Letter Cards** *b, c, d, e, g, h, j, K, l, m, n, p, r, t, u*

Building Words

▶ Word Families: *-ug, -ut, -en*

Display all the Letter Cards in a pocket chart. Tell children you want their help in building some words.

- ■ Arrange children in groups of three. Have the first group come to the pocket chart.

- ■ Say to the group: *Each of you should hold one card. Stand together to make the word* hug *for everyone to read.*

- ■ Say to the class: *You think about the sounds and see if this group chooses the letters you would choose.*

- ■ Coach the group as necessary, and then have the class blend the word as you point to the letters. Begin a list of all the words from this activity.

- ■ Now ask the same small group to change their word to *jug*. Continue in the same way, occasionally switching groups and building words from the *-ut* and *-en* families.

- ■ Conclude by cutting apart all the words on your list. Shuffle the words and give several to each small group, asking them to sort the words into families.

- ■ Children can write *-ug, -ut,* and *-en* words on index cards and add them to their personal word files. Suggest that children draw pictures on the backs to help them remember the words.

hug	cut	pen
rug	jut	men
bug	hut	hen
tug	nut	den
dug	rut	Ken
lug		ten
jug		
mug		

Sunshine State Standards pp. T150–T151   ★ = FCAT Benchmark in Gr. 3–5

★**LA.A.1.1.2.K.5** basic phonetic principles   **LA.B.1.1.2.K.3** able to sequence events
★**LA.A.1.1.3.K.4** uses sources to build vocabulary   **LA.B.2.1.1.K.2** ideas to shared writing
LA.B.1.1.2.K.1 dictates messages

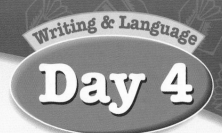

Interactive Writing

LA.B.1.1.2.K.1, 3

▶ ## Writing Directions

Viewing and Speaking Remind children that they have been using order words to tell *when* to do certain things.

■ Display the charts from previous writing activities. (See pages T125, T135, and T143.) Review the sequence of steps, and discuss the pet care chores.

■ Choose a new pet. Ask children to imagine that they have to leave clear directions for someone else to follow.

■ Brainstorm a list of chores, and list them on chart paper. Have children decide the order in which the steps should be followed.

■ Cut the chart into sentence strips, and order the strips with children. Add order words as needed.

■ As you rewrite the directions, invite volunteers to write known words. When patterned words are used, ask the class to tell you what letters to write at the end of each word. Have children write capital letters and add end punctuation marks.

At Group Time

Writing Center

LA.B.2.1.1.K.2
LA.B.1.1.2.K.3

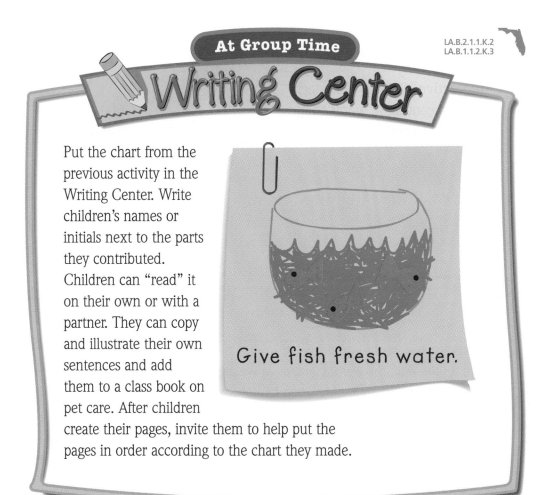

Put the chart from the previous activity in the Writing Center. Write children's names or initials next to the parts they contributed. Children can "read" it on their own or with a partner. They can copy and illustrate their own sentences and add them to a class book on pet care. After children create their pages, invite them to help put the pages in order according to the chart they made.

Give fish fresh water.

DAY 4

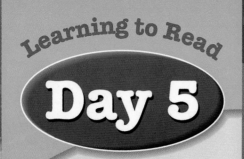

Learning to Read

Day 5

Day at a Glance

Learning to Read

Revisiting the Literature:

Run Away!, Henny Penny, Splash!, Feathers for Lunch, Which Pet?, Baby Animals Play, "The Bug Hut"

☑ **Phonics:** *-ug* and *-ut* Words; *page T156*

Word Work

Building Words, *page T158*

Writing & Language

Independent Writing, *page T159*

Managing Small Groups

Teacher-Led Group
- Reread familiar **Phonics Library** selections.
- Begin *Practice Book, 312,* **Blackline Master 36.**

Independent Groups
- Reread **Phonics Library** selections.
- Finish *Practice Book, 312,* **Blackline Master 36.**
- Centers

Opening

LA.A.2.1.5.K.2
★LA.A.1.1.2.K.6
★LA.A.1.1.3.K.4

Calendar

Sunday	Monday	Tuesday	Wednesday	Thursday	Friday	Saturday
			1	2	3	4
5	6	7	8	9	10	11
12	13	14	15	16	17	18
19	20	21	22	23	24	25
26	27	28	29	30	31	

Ask children to say the name of the day with you. Brainstorm animal names that begin with the same letter sound as the name of the day.

Daily Message

Interactive Writing Volunteers can help contribute words they can read and write.

Today we will choose our favorite book about animals.

Rearrange the words on the Word Wall. Then play a game: *I'm thinking of a word on the wall; the word is* are, *as in* We are reading. *I am going to point to some words on the wall. Clap when I point to the word* are. Point to several "wrong" words before the correct one. Continue with other words.

Routines

 ## Daily Phonemic Awareness
Blending and Segmenting Phonemes

- Stack the Picture Cards *bug, cat, dog, goat, hen, pig, seal*, and *yak* face down. Choose a card, but don't reveal the picture.

- *I'll say the sounds in this animal's name: / y / / a / / k /. Raise your hand when you know what it is.*

- After several cards, have children take turns being the leader, who says the separate sounds for others to blend. Add more Picture Cards to give everyone a turn.

 ## Phoneme Substitution

Have children sit in a circle. Hold up the *yak* card and turn to the child next to you. Ask: *What would* yak *be if I changed the first sound to / m /?* The child says *mak* and then turns to the next player and asks the same question, using a new sound. After a round, change "first sound" to "last sound" and continue.

Sunshine State Standards pp. T152–T153
★ = FCAT Benchmark in Gr. 3–5
★**LA.A.1.1.2.K.5** basic phonetic principles
★**LA.A.1.1.2.K.6** print conveys meaning
★**LA.A.1.1.3.K.4** uses sources to build vocabulary
LA.A.2.1.5.K.2 pictures, signs for information
LA.C.1.1.4.K.1 listens for specific information

Getting Ready to Learn

To help plan their day, tell children that they will

- reread and talk about all the books they've read during this theme.

- take home a story they can read.

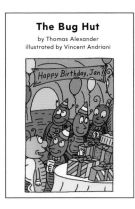

The Bug Hut
by Thomas Alexander
illustrated by Vincent Andriani

- write some directions in their journals.

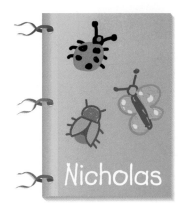

Nicholas

DAY 5

LA.B.2.1.3.K.1

www.eduplace.com

Log on to **Education Place** for more activities relating to *A World of Animals*.

www.bookadventure.org

This Internet reading-incentive program provides thousands of titles for children to read.

★LA.A.2.1.1.K.1
LA.C.3.1.2.K.1
★LA.A.1.1.2.K.5
LA.A.1.1.4.K.1
★LA.E.1.1.2.K.1

Revisiting the Literature

▶ ## Literature Discussion

Today, help children compare the literature you shared in this theme:

- Have volunteers show the animals in the Link *Which Pet?* that they liked best. Ask what made these pets interesting to them.

- Have someone summarize why the characters were running in *Run Away!* and in *Henny Penny.*

- Have children tell the important events in *The Tale of the Three Little Pigs.* Encourage children to use the words *first, next, then,* and *last* (or *finally*) to tell about the events in order.

- Have several children point out their favorite birds in *Feathers for Lunch.* Ask why the cat did not catch one.

- Together, read the title "The Bug Hut." Ask volunteers how they blended *Bug* and *Hut.*

- Talk about whether a character learned a lesson in any of the selections. How else were some of the stories alike?

Together, choose a favorite book to share again.

✓ ## Comprehension Focus:

Story Structure: Plot Remind children that they have learned to think about the important events in a story, including the problem and the solution. Display the pieces of fiction you have read during the theme, and ask children to name some of the important things that happened.

Sunshine State Standards pp. T154–T155   ★ = FCAT Benchmark in Gr. 3–5

★**LA.A.1.1.2.K.5** basic phonetic principles   LA.A.1.1.1.K.1 oral predictions
★**LA.A.2.1.1.K.1** main idea from a read-aloud   LA.A.1.1.4.K.1 strategies to comprehend text
★**LA.E.1.1.2.K.1** sequence of events, setting   LA.A.2.1.2.K.1 reads for pleasure

LA.A.1.1.1.K.1
LA.A.1.1.4.K.1
LA.A.2.1.2.K.1
LA.E.2.1.1.K.1

Animals at Play
by Wil Perry

Houghton Mifflin

Animals at Play

On My Way Practice Reader

▶ Preparing to Read

Building Background Share the title, and call attention to the word *Animals*. Ask children to tell about pets or other animals they have seen at play. Explain that this is an information book about many kinds of animals and how they play.

▶ Guiding the Reading

Invite children to comment on the photographs in the selection. Use the ideas below to prepare children for reading on their own.

page 1: *How can I tell that the first sentence is a question? Let's read it together... When you read this book, look for the answer. Have you ever played tug of war with a puppy and its toys?*

pages 2–3: *These pages show animals in different places. Where are they? How are the animals playing? Have you ever seen a pigpen? Who dug the pit where the pig is sitting? Why?*

pages 4–5: *How does a squirrel get from one tree branch to another? What will the fish do when the man cuts them out of the net?*

page 8: *How are the bears playing? Have you ever heard the words* bear hug? *What does that mean?*

Prompting Strategies Listen and observe children as they "whisper read," and use prompts such as these to help them apply strategies:

■ *That word is on the Word Wall. Can you find it and read it?*

■ *Read that line again and say the first sound in the word that gave you trouble. Can you blend all the sounds?*

■ *Would that word make sense in a sentence about this animal?*

▶ Responding

Have children brainstorm a list of other animals at play. Each child can draw and write about one type. Compile the pages into a new book for children to enjoy in the Book Center.

Leveled Books

The materials listed below provide reading practice for children at different levels.

Little Big Books

Feathers for Lunch

Splash!
Flora McDonnell

Little Readers for Guided Reading

Houghton Mifflin Classroom Bookshelf

LA.B.2.1.3.K.1 uses computer for writing
LA.C.3.1.2.K.1 asks, responds to questions
LA.E.2.1.1.K.1 relates own life to a read-aloud

★LA.A.1.1.2.K.2, 3, 5

Phonics Review

☑ Consonants, Word Families

OBJECTIVES

Children

- make and read words with initial consonants and short *u* + *g*, short *u* + *t*
- make sentences with high-frequency words

MATERIALS

- **Word Cards** *a, and, are, for, go, have, he, here, I, is, like, my, play, said, see, she, to, the*
- **Punctuation Cards:** period, question mark
- **Picture Cards** assorted

▶ Review

Tell children that today, the word readers will have to pay close attention to the word builders! Have a group of word builders stand with you at the chalkboard. Whisper the word *bug* to each one and have them write it on the board. If necessary, prompt them to quietly stretch out the sounds and write a letter for each one.

■ The word builders call on classmates (word readers) to identify the word. On chart paper, begin a list of words from this activity.

■ Now quietly tell the word builders to change one letter to change *bug* to *but.*

■ After the word is identified, have a new group change places with the first one. At your direction, they write *-ug, -ut,* and *-en* words you name at random and ask the word readers to identify them.

■ Continue until everyone builds a few words.

Now have children form small groups. Call attention to your word list. Cut out the words, give several to each small group, and ask them to sort the words into families. Check children's responses. Then collect the words, shuffle them, and repeat the activity.

Sunshine State Standards pp. T156–T157   ★ = FCAT Benchmark in Gr. 3–5

★**LA.A.1.1.2.K.2** knows alphabet   ★**LA.A.1.1.2.K.5** basic phonetic principles
★**LA.A.1.1.2.K.3** knows sounds of alphabet   ★**LA.A.1.1.3.K.1** identifies high-frequency words

★LA.A.1.1.3.K.1

High-Frequency Word Review

✔️ *I, see, my, like, a, to, and, go, is, here, for, have, said, play, she, are, he*

▶ Review

Give each small group the Word Cards, Picture Cards, and Punctuation Cards needed to make a sentence. Each child holds one card. Children stand and arrange themselves to make a sentence for others to read.

He | and | I | go | to | the | 🌿 | .

Is | she | at | the | 🌿 | ?

▶ Apply

Practice Book page 312 Children can complete this page independently and read it to you during small group time.

Phonics Library Have children take turns reading aloud to the class. Each child might read one page of "The Bug Hut" or a favorite **Phonics Library** selection from the previous theme. Remind readers to share the pictures!

Discussion questions:

■ *Do you hear any rhyming words in the story? What letters are the same in those words?*

■ *Find a word in "The Bug Hut" that begins with the same sound as* Jumping Jill. *What is the letter? What is the sound?*

■ *We added the words* are *and* he *to the Word Wall. Find those words in "The Bug Hut."*

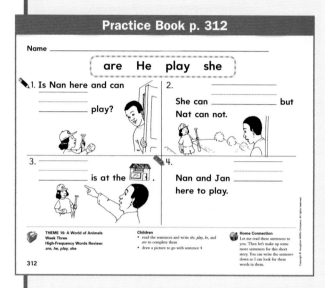

Practice Book p. 312

Name _____

| are | He | play | she |

1. Is Nan here and can _____ play?

2. She can _____ but Nat can not.

3. _____ is at the 🏠.

4. Nan and Jan _____ here to play.

THEME 10: A World of Animals
Week Three
High-Frequency Words Review:
are, he, play, she

Children
• read the sentences and write *she, play, he,* and *are* to complete them
• draw a picture to go with sentence 4

Home Connection
Let me read these sentences to you. Then let's make up some more sentences for this short story. You can write the sentence down so I can look for these words in them.

312

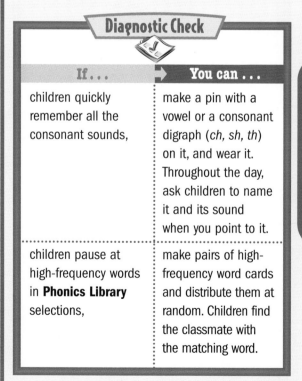

Diagnostic Check

If...	➤ You can...
children quickly remember all the consonant sounds,	make a pin with a vowel or a consonant digraph (*ch, sh, th*) on it, and wear it. Throughout the day, ask children to name it and its sound when you point to it.
children pause at high-frequency words in **Phonics Library** selections,	make pairs of high-frequency word cards and distribute them at random. Children find the classmate with the matching word.

DAY 5

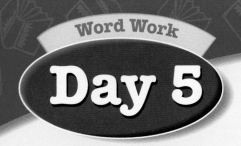

Day 5

Building Words

▶ Word Families: -ug, -ut, -en, -et, -ot

Tell children you want to build *bug* in the pocket chart. Ask what letters you need, prompting children as necessary to think about the sounds. Continue with *hen, wet, cut,* and *pot.* Write each word on an index card.

Now tell children you want them to help you use those words to build families of rhyming words. Have children sit in a circle. Give each one a small self-stick note and a crayon.

Hold up the index card for *bug* and read it. Then put a self-stick note over the *b* and write *t.* Hand the card to the next person and ask, ***What word do I make when I change the b in bug to t? Everyone think of the answer, but [Karen] will say it.*** The child responds, writes a new letter to cover yours, passes the card to the next player, and repeats the question with the appropriate letters. Play continues until no one can think of another word in that family.

Continue the activity with *-ut, -en, et,* and *-ot* words.

Have small groups work together to build families of *-ug, -ut, -en, -et,* and *-ot* words with stamps or letter tiles. They can add any new words to the Word Bank section of their journals and add appropriate pictures.

OBJECTIVES

Children
• build and read *-ug, -ut, -en, -et,* and *-ot* words

MATERIALS
• **Letter Cards** *b, c, e, g, h, n, o, p, t, u, w*

Sunshine State Standards pp. T158–T159   ★ = FCAT Benchmark in Gr. 3–5

★**LA.A.1.1.2.K.5** basic phonetic principles
★**LA.A.1.1.3.K.4** uses sources to build vocabulary
LA.B.2.1.1.K.1 uses pictures, words

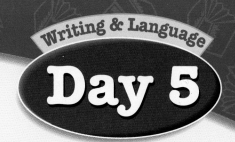
Independent Writing

LA.B.2.1.1.K.1

Journals Together, reread this week's shared and interactive writing posted in the classroom. Point out all the animal words and order words used to tell about animal and pet care. Tell children that today they will write directions for doing something.

■ Pass out the journals.

■ *Let's talk about taking care of animals. What do pets need in order to live? What do pets like to do? If you wanted to make some notes to remind yourself how to feed the neighbor's cat, what would you say to do first? What would you say to do next? What other types of directions could you write in your journal?*

■ You might provide different materials for children to illustrate their work, such as animal stamps or preprinted sheets for numbered "to do" lists.

■ If time permits, allow children to share what they've written with the class.

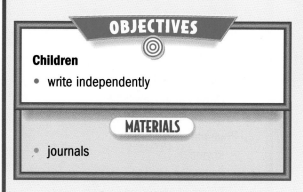

OBJECTIVES

Children
• write independently

MATERIALS
• journals

Teacher's Note

Suggest that children discuss their writing with you or a partner as they work. This will help them expand upon their ideas and add clarity.

Portfolio Opportunity

Have children browse through their journals and mark their favorite entries. Encourage children to explain their choices.

Theme Assessment Wrap-Up

Emerging Literacy Survey

Areas Assessed:

(1.) Concepts of Print
- Letter name knowledge
- Sound-letter association

(2.) Phonemic Awareness
- Rhyme
- Beginning sounds
- Blending onsets and rimes
- Segmenting onsets and rimes
- Blending phonemes
- Segmenting phonemes

(3.) Beginning Reading and Writing
- Word recognition
- Word writing
- Sentence dictation
- Oral reading

▷ Monitoring Literacy Development

If you have administered the **Emerging Literacy Survey** as a baseline assessment of the skills children brought with them to Kindergarten, this might be a good time to re-administer all or part of it to chart progress, to identify areas of strength and need, and to test the need for early intervention.

Use the **Observation Checklist** throughout the theme to write notes indicating whether each child has a beginning, developing, or proficient understanding of reading, writing, and language concepts. (See facing page.)

▷ Assessing Student Progress

Formal Assessment The **Integrated Theme Test** and the **Theme Skills Test** are formal assessments used to evaluate children's performance on theme objectives.

- The **Florida Integrated Theme Test** assesses children's progress as readers and writers in a format that reflects instruction. Simple decodable texts test reading skills in context.

- The **Theme Skills Test** assesses children's mastery of specific reading and language arts skills taught in the theme.

LA.A.1.1.1.K.1
LA.A.1.1.4.K.1
LA.A.2.1.2.K.1
LA.E.2.1.1.K.1

 MEETING INDIVIDUAL NEEDS

Animals at Play

On My Way Practice Reader

Animals at Play
by Wil Perry

Houghton Mifflin

▶ Preparing to Read

Building Background Share the title, and call attention to the word *Animals*. Ask children to tell about pets or other animals they have seen at play. Explain that this is an information book about many kinds of animals and how they play.

▶ Guiding the Reading

Invite children to comment on the photographs in the selection. Use the ideas below to prepare children for reading on their own.

page 1: *How can I tell that the first sentence is a question? Let's read it together... When you read this book, look for the answer. Have you ever played tug of war with a puppy and its toys?*

pages 2–3: *These pages show animals in different places. Where are they? How are the animals playing? Have you ever seen a pigpen? Who dug the pit where the pig is sitting? Why?*

pages 4–5: *How does a squirrel get from one tree branch to another? What will the fish do when the man cuts them out of the net?*

page 8: *How are the bears playing? Have you ever heard the words* bear hug? *What does that mean?*

Prompting Strategies Listen and observe children as they "whisper read," and use prompts such as these to help them apply strategies:

■ *That word is on the Word Wall. Can you find it and read it?*

■ *Read that line again and say the first sound in the word that gave you trouble. Can you blend all the sounds?*

■ *Would that word make sense in a sentence about this animal?*

▶ Responding

Have children brainstorm a list of other animals at play. Each child can draw and write about one type. Compile the pages into a new book for children to enjoy in the Book Center.

Leveled Books

The materials listed below provide reading practice for children at different levels.

Little Big Books

Reading
Feathers for Lunch

Reading
Splash!
Flora McDonnell

Little Readers for Guided Reading

LITTLE READERS
FOR GUIDED READING

Houghton Mifflin Classroom Bookshelf

Katy No-Pocket
MY FRIEND and I
Sheep in a Jeep
Do Pigs Have Stripes?

DAY 5

LA.B.2.1.3.K.1 uses computer for writing
LA.C.3.1.2.K.1 asks, responds to questions
LA.E.2.1.1.K.1 relates own life to a read-aloud

Revisiting the Literature/ Building Fluency

T155

★LA.A.1.1.2.K.2, 3, 5

Phonics Review

✓ Consonants, Word Families

OBJECTIVES

Children

- make and read words with initial consonants and short *u* + *g*, short *u* + *t*
- make sentences with high-frequency words

MATERIALS

- **Word Cards** *a, and, are, for, go, have, he, here, I, is, like, my, play, said, see, she, to, the*
- **Punctuation Cards:** period, question mark
- **Picture Cards** assorted

▶ Review

Tell children that today, the word readers will have to pay close attention to the word builders! Have a group of word builders stand with you at the chalkboard. Whisper the word *bug* to each one and have them write it on the board. If necessary, prompt them to quietly stretch out the sounds and write a letter for each one.

- ■ The word builders call on classmates (word readers) to identify the word. On chart paper, begin a list of words from this activity.

- ■ Now quietly tell the word builders to change one letter to change *bug* to *but*.

- ■ After the word is identified, have a new group change places with the first one. At your direction, they write -*ug*, -*ut*, and -*en* words you name at random and ask the word readers to identify them.

- ■ Continue until everyone builds a few words.

Now have children form small groups. Call attention to your word list. Cut out the words, give several to each small group, and ask them to sort the words into families. Check children's responses. Then collect the words, shuffle them, and repeat the activity.

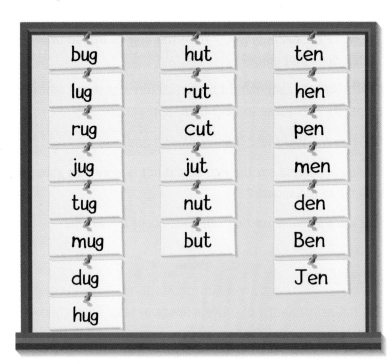

Sunshine State Standards pp. T156–T157   ★ = FCAT Benchmark in Gr. 3–5

★LA.A.1.1.2.K.2 knows alphabet   ★LA.A.1.1.2.K.5 basic phonetic principles
★LA.A.1.1.2.K.3 knows sounds of alphabet   ★LA.A.1.1.3.K.1 identifies high-frequency words

★LA.A.1.1.3.K.1

High-Frequency Word Review

✓ *I, see, my, like, a, to, and, go, is, here, for, have, said, play, she, are, he*

▶ Review

Give each small group the Word Cards, Picture Cards, and Punctuation Cards needed to make a sentence. Each child holds one card. Children stand and arrange themselves to make a sentence for others to read.

He   and   I   go   to   the   🌿   .

Is   she   at   the   🌿   ?

▶ Apply

Practice Book page 312 Children can complete this page independently and read it to you during small group time.

Phonics Library Have children take turns reading aloud to the class. Each child might read one page of "The Bug Hut" or a favorite **Phonics Library** selection from the previous theme. Remind readers to share the pictures!

Discussion questions:

- *Do you hear any rhyming words in the story? What letters are the same in those words?*

- *Find a word in "The Bug Hut" that begins with the same sound as* Jumping Jill. *What is the letter? What is the sound?*

- *We added the words* are *and* he *to the Word Wall. Find those words in "The Bug Hut."*

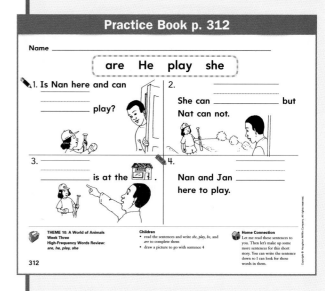
Diagnostic Check

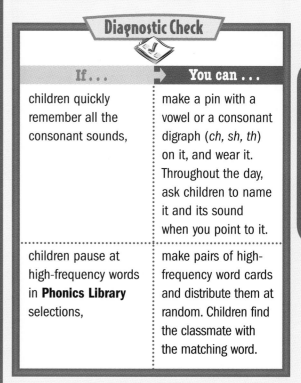

If . . .	▶ You can . . .
children quickly remember all the consonant sounds,	make a pin with a vowel or a consonant digraph (*ch, sh, th*) on it, and wear it. Throughout the day, ask children to name it and its sound when you point to it.
children pause at high-frequency words in **Phonics Library** selections,	make pairs of high-frequency word cards and distribute them at random. Children find the classmate with the matching word.

DAY 5

Day 5

OBJECTIVES

Children

- build and read -ug, -ut, -en, -et, and -ot words

MATERIALS

- **Letter Cards** b, c, e, g, h, n, o, p, t, u, w

Building Words

▶ Word Families: -ug, -ut, -en, -et, -ot

Tell children you want to build *bug* in the pocket chart. Ask what letters you need, prompting children as necessary to think about the sounds. Continue with *hen, wet, cut,* and *pot.* Write each word on an index card.

Now tell children you want them to help you use those words to build families of rhyming words. Have children sit in a circle. Give each one a small self-stick note and a crayon.

Hold up the index card for *bug* and read it. Then put a self-stick note over the *b* and write *t.* Hand the card to the next person and ask, ***What word do I make when I change the** b **in** bug **to** t? **Everyone think of the answer, but [Karen] will say it.*** The child responds, writes a new letter to cover yours, passes the card to the next player, and repeats the question with the appropriate letters. Play continues until no one can think of another word in that family.

Continue the activity with *-ut, -en, et,* and *-ot* words.

Have small groups work together to build families of *-ug, -ut, -en, -et,* and *-ot* words with stamps or letter tiles. They can add any new words to the Word Bank section of their journals and add appropriate pictures.

Sunshine State Standards pp. T158–T159   ★ = FCAT Benchmark in Gr. 3–5

★**LA.A.1.1.2.K.5** basic phonetic principles
★**LA.A.1.1.3.K.4** uses sources to build vocabulary
LA.B.2.1.1.K.1 uses pictures, words

Observation Checklist

Name _____   Date _____

	Beginning	Developing	Proficient
Listening Comprehension • Participates in shared and choral reading			
• Listens to story attentively			
Phonemic Awareness • Blends, segments phonemes			
• Substitutes phonemes			
• Identifies beginning sound			
Phonics • Recognizes sound for *j*			
• Builds words with word families *-ug, -ut*			
Concepts of Print • Uses a capital at the beginning of a sentence			
• Uses end punctuation (period, question mark, exclamation mark)			
Reading • Reads simple texts			
• Reads the high-frequency words *are, he*			
Comprehension • Identifies story beginning, middle, and end			
• Recognizes plot (problem/ solution)			
• Can compare and contrast story elements			
Writing and Language • Writes simple phrases and sentences			
• Participates in shared and interactive writing			

For each child, write notes or checkmarks in the appropriate columns.

Theme Resources

Resources for *A World of Animals*

Contents

Twinkle, Twinkle, Little Star

Moderately

Jumping Jill

(Tune: "Twinkle, Twinkle, Little Star")

Jumping Jill can jump
    so high.

Jill can jump in warm July.

Jumping Jill can jump
    so low.

Jill can jump for joy,
    you know.

Join her in a jumping game.

As you jump, call out her name!

Use this music for Jumping Jill's song.

Down in the Valley

Plaintively

Folk Song

Umbie Umbrella's Song

Umbie Umbrella keeps us dry in the rain.
Umbie Umbrella will never complain.
We stand under Umbie, until we see sun.
Then we thank Umbie for a job that's well done.

Use this music for Umbie Umbrella's song.

Word List

In Themes 1 through 3, the Phonics Library stories are wordless.

Theme 1

▶ **Phonics Skills:** none taught in this theme
▶ **High-Frequency Words:** none taught in this theme

Phonics Library, Week 1:
We Go to School
  wordless story

Phonics Library, Week 2:
See What We Can Do
  wordless story

Phonics Library, Week 3:
We Can Make It
  wordless story

Theme 2

▶ **Phonics Skills:** Initial consonants s, m, r
▶ **High-Frequency Words:** I, see

Phonics Library, Week 1:
My Red Boat
  wordless story
Phonics Library, Week 2:
Look at Me
  wordless story

Phonics Library, Week 3:
The Parade
  wordless story

Theme 3

▶ **Phonics Skills:** Initial consonants t, b, n
▶ **High-Frequency Words:** my, like

Phonics Library, Week 1:
The Birthday Party
  wordless story

Phonics Library, Week 2:
Baby Bear's Family
  wordless story

Phonics Library, Week 3:
Cat's Surprise
  wordless story

Theme 4

▶ **Phonics Skills:** Initial consonants h, v, c; words with -at
▶ **High-Frequency Words:** a, to

Phonics Library, Week 1:
Nat at Bat
  Words with -at: at, bat, hat, Nat, sat
  High-Frequency Words: my, see

Phonics Library, Week 2:
A Vat
  Words with -at: hat, mat, rat, vat
  High-Frequency Word: a

Phonics Library, Week 3:
Cat Sat
  Words with -at: bat, cat, hat, mat, sat
  High-Frequency Words: my, see

Theme 5

▶ **Phonics Skills:** Initial consonants p, g, f; words with -an
▶ **High-Frequency Words:** and, go

Phonics Library, Week 1:
Nat, Pat, and Nan
  Words with -an: Nan, ran
  Words with -at: Nat, Pat, sat
  High-Frequency Words: and, see

Phonics Library, Week 2:
Go, Cat!
  Words with -an: Nan, ran, Van
  Words with -at: Cat, Pat, sat
  High-Frequency Word: go

Phonics Library, Week 3:
Pat and Nan
  Words with -an: fan, Nan, ran
  Words with -at: Pat, sat
  High-Frequency Words: a, and, go

Theme 6

▶ **Phonics Skills:** Initial consonants l, k, qu; words with -it
▶ **High-Frequency Words:** is, here

Phonics Library, Week 1:
Can It Fit?
  Words with -it: fit, it, sit
  Words with -an: can, man, van
  High-Frequency Words: a, go, I, is, my

Phonics Library, Week 2:
Kit
  Words with -it: bit, fit, it, Kit, lit, sit
  Words with -an: can, pan
  Words with -at: hat
  High-Frequency Words: a, here, I

Phonics Library, Week 3:
Fan
  Words with -it: bit, quit
  Words with -an: an, Fan
  Words with -at: sat
  High-Frequency Words: a, here, is

Theme 7

▶ **Phonics Skills:** Initial consonants d, z; words with -ig
▶ **High-Frequency Words:** for, have

Phonics Library, Week 1:
Big Rig
  Words with -ig: Big, dig, Rig
  Words with -it: pit
  Words with -an: can, Dan
  High-Frequency Words: a, for

Phonics Library, Week 2:
Tan Van
  Words with -ig: Pig, Zig
  Words with -it: it
  Words with -an: can, Dan, ran, tan, van
  Words with -at: Cat, sat
  High-Frequency Words: a, have, I, is

Phonics Library, Week 3:
Zig Pig and Dan Cat
  Words with -ig: dig, Pig, Zig
  Words with -it: it
  Words with -an: can, Dan
  Words with -at: Cat, sat
  High-Frequency Words: and, for, have, here, I, is

Theme 8

- ➤ **Phonics Skills:** Consonant x; words with -ot, -ox
- ➤ **High-Frequency Words:** said, the

Phonics Library, Week 1:
Dot Got a Big Pot

Words with -ot: Dot, got, hot, lot, pot
Words with -ig: big
Words with -it: it
Words with -an: Nan
Words with -at: Nat, sat
High-Frequency Words: a, and, I, is, like, said

Phonics Library, Week 2:
The Big, Big Box

Words with -ox: box, Fox
Words with -ot: not
Words with -ig: big
Words with -it: bit, fit, hit, it
Words with -an: can, Dan, Fan
Words with -at: Cat, hat, mat, sat
High-Frequency Words: a, is, my, said, the

Phonics Library, Week 3:
A Pot for Dan Cat

Words with -ot: pot
Words with -ox: Fox
Words with -ig: big
Words with -it: fit
Words with -an: can, Dan, Fan, ran
Words with -at: Cat, sat
High-Frequency Words: a, and, see, said

Theme 9

- ➤ **Phonics Skills:** Initial consonants w, y; words with -et, -en
- ➤ **High-Frequency Words:** play, she

Phonics Library, Week 1:
Get Set! Play!

Words with -et: get, set, wet, yet
Words with -ot: got, not
Words with -ox: Fox
Words with -ig: Pig
Words with -an: can
High-Frequency Words: a, play, said

Phonics Library, Week 2:
Ben

Words with -en: Ben, Hen, men, ten
Words with -et: get, net, pet, vet, yet
Words with -ot: got, not
Words with -ox: box, Fox
Words with -it: it
Words with -an: can
High-Frequency Words: a, I, my, play, said, she, the

Phonics Library, Week 3:
Pig Can Get Wet

Words with -et: get, wet
Words with -ot: got, not
Words with -ig: big, Pig, wig
Words with -it: sit
Words with -an: can
Words with -at: Cat, sat
High-Frequency Words: a, my, play, said, she

Theme 10

- ➤ **Phonics Skills:** Initial consonant j; words with -ug, -ut
- ➤ **High-Frequency Words:** are, he

Phonics Library, Week 1:
Ken and Jen

Words with -ug: dug
Words with -en: Ken, Jen
Words with -et: wet
Words with -ot: hot
Words with -ig: big, dig
Words with -it: it, pit
High-Frequency Words: a, and, are, is

Phonics Library, Week 2:
It Can Fit

Words with -ut: but, nut
Words with -ug: jug, lug, rug
Words with -ox: box
Words with -ot: not
Words with -ig: big
Words with -it: fit, it
Words with -an: can, tan, van
Words with -at: fat, hat
High-Frequency Words: a, he, see, she

Phonics Library, Week 3:
The Bug Hut

Words with -ut: but
Words with -ug: Bug, hug, lug
Words with -ox: box
Words with -ot: Dot, got, not
Words with -ig: Big, jig
Words with -an: can, Jan
Words with -at: fat, hat
High-Frequency Words: a, here, is, she, the

Cumulative Word List

By the end of Theme 10, children will have been taught the skills necessary to read the following words.

Words with -at
at, bat, cat, fat, hat, mat, Nat, Pat, rat, sat, vat

Words with -an
an, ban, can, Dan, fan, Jan, man, Nan, pan, ran, tan, van

Words with -it
bit, fit, hit, it, kit, lit, pit, quit, sit, wit

Words with -ig
big, dig, fig, jig, pig, rig, wig, zig

Words with -ot
cot, dot, got, hot, jot, lot, not, pot, rot, tot

Words with -ox
box, fox, ox

Words with -et
bet, get, jet, let, met, net, pet, set, vet, wet, yet

Words with -en
Ben, den, hen, Jen, Ken, men, pen, ten

Words with -ug
bug, dug, hug, jug, lug, mug, rug, tug

Words with -ut
but, cut, hut, jut, nut, rut

High-Frequency Words
a, and, are, for, go, have, he, here, I, is, like, my, play, said, see, she, the, to

Technology Resources

American Melody
P. O. Box 270
Guilford, CT 06473
800-220-5557

Audio Bookshelf
174 Prescott Hill Road
Northport, ME 04849
800-234-1713

Baker & Taylor
100 Business Court Drive
Pittsburgh, PA 15205
800-775-2600

BDD Audio
1540 Broadway
New York, NY 10036
800-223-6834

Big Kids Productions
1606 Dywer Avenue
Austin, TX 78704
800-477-7811
www.bigkidsvideo.com

Blackboard Entertainment
2647 International
Boulevard
Suite 853
Oakland, CA 94601
800-968-2261
www.blackboardkids.com

Books on Tape
P. O. Box 7900
Newport Beach, CA 92658
800-626-3333

Filmic Archives
The Cinema Center
Botsford, CT 06404
800-366-1920
www.filmicarchives.com

Great White Dog Picture Company
10 Toon Lane
Lee, NH 03824
800-397-7641
www.greatwhitedog.com

HarperAudio
10 E. 53rd Street
New York, NY 10022
800-242-7737

Houghton Mifflin Company
222 Berkeley Street
Boston, MA 02116
800-225-3362

Informed Democracy
P. O. Box 67
Santa Cruz, CA 95063
831-426-3921

JEF Films
143 Hickory Hill Circle
Osterville, MA 02655
508-428-7198

Kimbo Educational
P. O. Box 477
Long Branch, NJ 07740
900-631-2187

The Learning Company (dist. for Broderbund)
1 Athenaeum Street
Cambridge, MA 02142
800-716-8506
www.learningcompa-
nyschool.com

Library Video Co.
P. O. Box 580
Wynnewood, PA 19096
800-843-3620

Listening Library
One Park Avenue
Old Greenwich, CT 06870
800-243-4504

Live Oak Media
P. O. Box 652
Pine Plains, NY 12567
800-788-1121
liveoak@taconic.net

Media Basics
Lighthouse Square
P. O. Box 449
Guilford, CT 06437
800-542-2505
www.mediabasicsvideo.com

Microsoft Corp.
One Microsoft Way
Redmond, WA 98052
800-426-9400
www.microsoft.com

National Geographic Society
1145 17th Street N. W.
Washington, D. C. 20036
800-368-2728
www.nationalgeographic.com

New Kid Home Video
1364 Palisades Beach Road
Santa Monica, CA 90401
310-451-5164

Puffin Books
345 Hudson Street
New York, NY 10014
212-366-2000

Rainbow Educational Media
4540 Preslyn Drive
Raleigh, NC 27616
800-331-4047

Random House Home Video
201 E. 50th Street
New York, NY 10022
212-940-7620

Recorded Books
270 Skipjack Road
Prince Frederick, MD 20678
800-638-1304
www.recordedbooks.com

Sony Wonder
Dist. by Professional
Media Service
19122 S. Vermont Avenue
Gardena, CA 90248
800-223-7672

Spoken Arts
8 Lawn Avenue
P. O. Box 100
New Rochelle, NY 10802
800-326-4090

SRA Media
220 E. Danieldale Road
DeSoto, TX 75115
800-843-8855

Sunburst Communications
101 Castleton Street
P. O. Box 100
Pleasantville, NY 10570
800-321-7511
www.sunburst.com

SVE & Churchill Media
6677 North Northwest
Highway
Chicago, IL 60631
800-829-1900

Tom Snyder Productions
80 Coolidge Hill Road
Watertown, MA 02472
800-342-0236
www.tomsnyder.com

Troll Communications
100 Corporate Drive
Mahwah, NJ 07430
800-526-5289

Weston Woods
12 Oakwood Avenue
Norwalk, CT 06850-1318
800-243-5020
www.scholastic.com

Index

Boldface page references indicate formal strategy and skill instruction.

E

English Language Learners, activities especially helpful for, *T42, T87, T96, T98*

background, building, *T10, T40*

Expanding literacy. *See* Skills links.

F

Fantasy and realism. *See* Comprehension skills.

Fluency

reading, *T49, T105*

G

Grammar and usage

speech, parts of. *See* Speech, parts of.

Graphic information, interpreting

calendars, *T8, T16, T26, T38, T46, T60, T70, T80, T94, T102, T116, T136, T144, T152*

Guided reading. *See* Coached reading.

H

Handwriting, *T21, T75*

High-frequency words

a, ***T14, T24, T51, T107***
and, ***T51, T107***
are, ***T22–T23, T51***
for, ***T51, T107***
go, ***T14, T51, T107***
have, ***T51, T107***
he, ***T76–T77, T78***
here, ***T51, T107***
I, ***T14, T51, T107***
is, ***T51, T107***
like, ***T51, T107***
my, ***T51, T107***
play, ***T51, T107***
said, ***T51, T107***
see, ***T14, T51, T107***
she, ***T51, T107***

the, ***T51***
to, ***T14, T51, T107***

Home connection, *xiii, T12, T35, T49, T66, T91, T105*

I

Independent and recreational reading. *See* Reading modes.

Independent writing

daily, *xiv*
suggestions for, *T109, T159*

Individual needs, meeting

Challenge, *T31, T41, T85, T97*
English Language Learners, *T10, T40, T42, T87, T96, T98*
Extra Support, *T19, T20, T28, T34, T62, T73, T74, T82, T90*

Inferences, making

predicting, *T62, T72, T83, T86, T96*

Informational selection, structure of. *See* Comprehension, text organization.

Information skills, *T25, T37*

Instructional routines, *xiv*

Interactive writing, *T8, T16, T26, T45, T60, T80, T94, T101, T150*

J

Journal, *xiv, T53, T109*

Judgments, making. *See* Comprehension skills.

K

Knowledge, activating prior. *See* Background, building.

L

Language and usage. *See* Speech, parts of.

Language concepts and skills

exact words, *T79*

Leveled books

Houghton Mifflin Classroom Bookshelf, *v, T49, T105*
Little Big Books, *v, T49, T105*
Little Readers for Guided Reading, *v, T49, T105*
On My Way Practice Reader, *v, T155*
Phonics Library, *v, T35, T43, T51, T91, T141*

Limited English proficient students. *See* English Language Learners.

Listening

for information, *T25*
for rhymes, *T79*
purpose
to compare sounds, *T13, T67*
to discriminate sounds, *T13, T67*
to an audiotape. *See* Audiotapes.
to a read aloud story. *See* Read Aloud selections.
to creative dramatics. *See* Creative dramatics.

Literature

comparing, *T104*
discussion. *See* Responding to literature.
responding to. *See* Responding to literature.
sharing, *T18–T19, T28–T32, T40–T41, T72–T73, T82–T89, T96–T97, T138–T139, T146–T147*

Locating information. *See* Information skills.

M

Main idea and supporting details, identifying. *See* Comprehension skills.

Mechanics, language. *See* Concepts of print.